Workshop on Unsupervised and Minimally Supervised Learning of Lexical Semantics 2009

Held at NAACL HLT 2009

Boulder, Colorado, USA
5 June 2009

ISBN: 978-1-61738-571-1

Printed from e-media with permission by:

Curran Associates, Inc.
57 Morehouse Lane
Red Hook, NY 12571
www.proceedings.com

Some format issues inherent in the e-media version may also appear in this print version.

Printed by Curran Associates, Inc. (2010)

Association for Computational Linguistics
209 N. Eighth Street
Stroudsburg, Pennsylvania 18360

Phone: 1-570-476-8006
Fax: 1-570-476-0860

acl@aclweb.org

Introduction

Lexical semantics (the semantics of words) has become an important part of Natural Language Processing due to its practical application in a number of areas such as machine translation, web & enterprise search, ontology learning etc.

This fact can be observed by looking at the increasing interest in the field of learning of lexical semantics e.g. the last Semantic Evaluation Workshop (SemEval-2007) consisted of 18 tasks ranging from the traditional Word Sense Disambiguation (WSD) task to the most recent of Word Sense Induction (WSI), web people search, metonymy resolution and others.

Given the wide variety of applications exploiting lexical semantics it is significant to focus on methods and techniques, which can overcome the "Knowledge Acquisition Bottleneck" and deal with the cost-prohibitive, error-prone and labor-intensive processes of creating hand-tagged training data.

The emphasis of this workshop is on unsupervised and minimally supervised methods relevant to learning of lexical semantics. The goal of this workshop is to provide a venue for researchers to obtain a better understanding on the issues and challenges that need to be tackled in order to overcome a number of significant problems within lexical semantics, such as data sparsity, unsupervised and minimally supervised parameter estimation, efficient and effective use of the web, and applications of distributional similarity.

We are very happy that the workshop has accepted a set of seven high quality papers tackling the above problems, and hope that their contribution will have an impact on the field. We are grateful to the program committee for their effort to thoroughly review the submissions. We would also like to thank Martha Palmer for presenting her noteworthy work in the workshop.

Suresh Manandhar & Ioannis P. Klapaftis
Co-chairs

Organizers

Suresh Manandhar, University of York, UK
Ioannis P. Klapaftis, University of York, UK

Program Committee

Eneko Agirre, University of the Basque Country, Spain
Enrique Alfonseca, Google, Switzerland
Chris Biemann, Powerset, USA
Philipp Cimiano, TU Delft, The Netherlands
James Cussens, University of York, UK
Cristian Danescu Niculescu-Mizil, Cornell University, USA
Aria Haghighi, University of California, Berkeley, USA
Nancy Ide, Vassar College, USA
Kyo Kaguera, University of Tokyo, Japan
Ioannis Klapaftis, University of York, UK
Lillian Lee, Cornell University, USA
Suresh Manandhar, University of York, UK
Ted Pedersen, University of Minnesota, USA
German Rigua, University of the Basque Country, Spain
Carlo Strapparava, ITC-Irst, Italy
Fangzhong Su, University of Leeds, UK
David Weir, University of Sussex, UK

Invited speakers

Martha Palmer, University of Colorado at Boulder, USA

Invited Talk

Knowing a Word(sense) by its company

Martha Palmer
University of Colorado at Boulder, USA

Abstract Supervised word sense disambiguation requires training corpora that have been tagged with word senses, and these word senses typically come from a pre-existing sense inventory. Space limitations imposed by dictionary publishers have biased the field towards lists of discrete senses for an individual lexeme. This approach does not capture information about relatedness of individual senses. How important is this information to knowing which sense distinctions are critical for particular types of NLP applications? How much does sense relatedness affect automatic word sense disambiguation performance? Recent psycholinguistic evidence seems to indicate that closely related word senses may be represented in the mental lexicon much like a single sense, whereas distantly related senses may be represented more like discrete entities. These results suggest that, for the purposes of WSD, closely related word senses can be clustered together into a more general sense with little meaning loss. This talk will describe the relatedness of verb senses and its impact on NLP applications and WSD components as well as recent psycholinguistic research results.

Table of Contents

Conference Program

Friday, June 5, 2009

9:15–9:30 Opening remarks

9:30–10:00 *Acquiring Applicable Common Sense Knowledge from the Web*
Hansen A. Schwartz and Fernando Gomez

10:00–10:30 *Utilizing Contextually Relevant Terms in Bilingual Lexicon Extraction*
Azniah Ismail and Suresh Manandhar

10:30–11:00 Morning break

11:00–12:00 Invited talk: Martha Palmer, Knowing a Word(sense) by its company

12:00–12:30 *Corpus-based Semantic Lexicon Induction with Web-based Corroboration*
Sean Igo and Ellen Riloff

12:30–14:00 Lunch break

14:00–14:30 *Cross-lingual Predicate Cluster Acquisition to Improve Bilingual Event Extraction by Inductive Learning*
Heng Ji

14:30–15:00 *Graph Connectivity Measures for Unsupervised Parameter Tuning of Graph-Based Sense Induction Systems.*
Ioannis Korkontzelos, Ioannis Klapaftis and Suresh Manandhar

15:00–15:30 *Combining Syntactic Co-occurrences and Nearest Neighbours in Distributional Methods to Remedy Data Sparseness.*
Lonneke van der Plas

15:30–16:00 Afternoon break

16:00–16:30 *Using DEDICOM for Completely Unsupervised Part-of-Speech Tagging*
Peter Chew, Brett Bader and Alla Rozovskaya

16:30–17:00 Closing remarks & discussion

Acquiring Applicable Common Sense Knowledge from the Web

Hansen A. Schwartz and Fernando Gomez
School of Electrical Engineering and Computer Science
University of Central Florida
Orlando, FL 32816, USA
{hschwartz, gomez}@cs.ucf.edu

Abstract

In this paper, a framework for acquiring common sense knowledge from the Web is presented. Common sense knowledge includes information about the world that humans use in their everyday lives. To acquire this knowledge, relationships between nouns are retrieved by using search phrases with automatically filled constituents. Through empirical analysis of the acquired nouns over WordNet, probabilities are produced for relationships between a concept and a word rather than between two words. A specific goal of our acquisition method is to acquire knowledge that can be successfully applied to NLP problems. We test the validity of the acquired knowledge by means of an application to the problem of word sense disambiguation. Results show that the knowledge can be used to improve the accuracy of a state of the art unsupervised disambiguation system.

1 Introduction

Common sense knowledge (*CSK*) is the knowledge we use in everyday life without necessarily being aware of it. Panton et al. (2006) of the Cyc project, define common sense as "the knowledge that every person assumes his neighbors also possess". Although the term common sense may be understood as a process such as reasoning, we are referring only to knowledge. It is *CSK* that tells us keys are kept in one's pocket and keys are used to open a door, but *CSK* does not hold that keys are kept in a kitchen sink or that keys are used to turn on a microwave, although all are possible.

To show the need for this information more clearly we provide a couple sentences:

She put the batter in the refrigerator. (1)
He ate the apple in the refrigerator. (2)

In (1), we are dealing with lexical ambiguity. There is little doubt for us to determine just what the "batter" is (food/substance used in baking). However, a computer must determine that it is not someone who swings a bat in baseball that is being put into a refrigerator, although it is entirely possible to do (depending on the size of the refrigerator). This demonstrates how *CSK* can be useful in solving *word sense disambiguation*. We know it is common for food to be found in a refrigerator and so we easily resolve batter as a food/substance rather than a person.

CSK can also help to solve syntactic ambiguity. The problem of *prepositional phrase attachment* occurs in sentences similar to (2). In this case, it is difficult for a computer to determine if "he" is in the refrigerator eating an apple or if the "apple" which he ate was in the refrigerator. Like the previous example, the knowledge that food is commonly found in a refrigerator and people are not, leads us to understand that "in the refrigerator" should be attached to the noun phrase "the apple" and not as a modifier of the verb phrase "ate".

Unfortunately, there are not many sources of *CSK* readily available for use in computer algorithms. Those sets of knowledge that are available, such as the CYC project (Lenat, 1995) or ConceptNet (Liu and Singh, 2004) rely on manually provided or crafted data. Our aim is to develop an automatic approach to acquire *CSK*[1] by turning to the vast amount of unannotated text that is available on the Web. In turn, we present a method to automatically retrieve and analyze phrases from the Web.

[1] data available at: http://eecs.ucf.edu/~hschwartz/CSK/

Proceedings of the NAACL HLT Workshop on Unsupervised and Minimally Supervised Learning of Lexical Semantics, pages 1–9,
Boulder, Colorado, June 2009. ©2009 Association for Computational Linguistics

We employ the use of a syntactic parser to accurately match syntactic patterns of phrases acquired from the Web. The data is analyzed over WordNet (Miller et al., 1993) in order to induce knowledge about word senses or concepts rather than words. Finally, we evaluate whether the knowledge by applying it to the problem of *word sense disambiguation.*

2 Background

The particular type of *CSK* that we experiment with in this paper is described formally as follows:

A relationship, *e1***R***e2*, exists between entities *e1* and *e2* if one finds "*e1* is **R** *e2*."

Some examples include: "a cup is on a table" and "food is in a refrigerator", which would result in relationships: *cup***on***table* and *food***in***refrigerator*. The next section attempts to make the relationship more clear, as we provide a brief linguistic background of prepositions and relationships.

2.1 Prepositions and Relationships

Prepositions state a relationship between two entities (Quirk et al., 1985). One of the entities is typically a constituent of the sentence while the other is the complement to the preposition. For example, consider the relationship between 'furniture' and 'house' in the following sentences:

The furniture is...
...at the house.
...on the house.
...in the house.

'The furniture' is the subject of the sentence, while 'the house' is a prepositional complement. Notice that the meaning is different for each sentence depending on the actual preposition ('at', 'on', or 'in'), and thus *furniture* relates to *house* in three different ways. Although each relationship between *furniture* and *house* is possible, only one would be considered *CSK* to most people: *furniture***in***house*.

We focus on prepositions which indicate a positive spacial relationship given by Quirk et al. (1985). There are three types of such relationships: "at a point", "on a line or surface", and "in an area or volume". In particular, we concentrate on the 1 to 3 dimensional relationships given in Table 1, denoted *on* and *in* throughout the paper. *At*, the 0 dimensional relationship, occurred far less frequently. The sentences below exemplify each of the 1 to 3 dimensional relationships:

dims	description	prepositions
1 or 2	*on* surface or line	on, onto, atop, upon, on top of, down on
2 or 3	*in* area or volume	in, into, inside, within, inside of

Table 1: Spatial dimensions (**dims**) and corresponding prepositions.

on surface	The keyboard is on the table.
on line	The beach is on US 1.
in area	The bank is in New York.
in volume	The vegetables are in the bowl.

2.2 Related Work

As a prevalent source of lexical knowledge, dictionary definitions may be regarded as common sense. However, some definitions may be considered expert knowledge rather than *CSK*. The scope of definitions certainly do not provide all necessary information (such as *keys are commonly kept in one's pocket*). We examine WordNet in particular because the hypernym relation has been developed extensively for nouns. The noun ontology is used in our work to help induce relationships involving concepts (senses of nouns) rather than just among words. This notion of inducing *CSK* among concepts, rather than words, is a key difference between our work and similar research.

The work on VerbOcean is similar to our research in the use of the Web for acquiring relationships (Chklovski and Pantel, 2004). They used patterns of phrases in order to search the Web for semantic relations among verbs. The knowledge they acquire falls into the category of *CSK*, but the specific relationships are different than ours in that they are among verb word forms and senses are not resolved.

ConceptNet was created based on the OpenMind Commonsense project (Liu and Singh, 2004). The project acquired knowledge through an interface on the Web by having users play games and answer questions about words. A contribution of ConceptNet is that it has a wide range of relations. While WordNet provides connections between concepts (senses of words), ConceptNet only provides relationships between word forms.

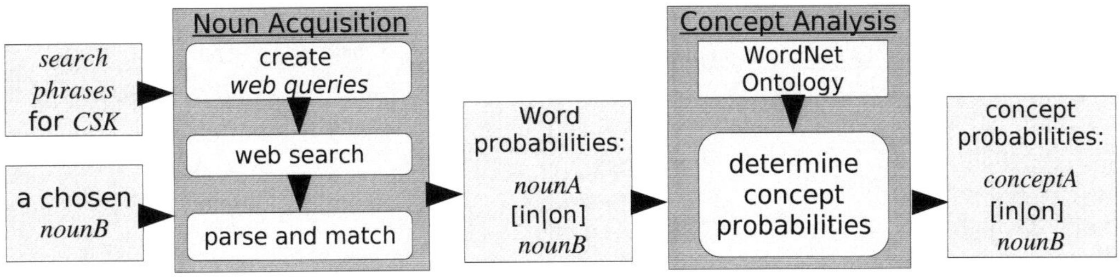

Figure 1: The overall *common sense knowledge* acquisition framework under the assumption that one is acquiring concepts (WordNet synsets) in a relationship with a given *nounB* (word).

A project in progress for over twenty years, CYC has been acquiring *common sense knowledge* about everyday objects and actions stored in 10^6 axioms (Lenat, 1995). The axioms, handcrafted by workers at CYCcorp, represent knowledge rooted in propositions. There are three layers of information: the first two, *access* and *physical*, contain meta data, while the third, *logical* layer, stores high level implicit meanings. Only a portion of CYC is available to the public.

Our method for acquiring knowledge is somewhat similar to that of (Hearst, 1992). Patterns are built manually. However, we do not use our manually constructed patterns (referred to as *search phrases*) to query the Web. Instead the *search phrases* are abstract patterns that are used to automatically generate more specific *web queries* by filling constituents based on lists of words.

The SemEval-2007 Task 4 presents a good overview of work in noun-noun relationships (Girju et al., 2007). Our work is related in that the relationships we acquire are between nominals, and in order to build their corpus Girju et al. queried the web with patterns like that of Hearst's work (Hearst, 1992). The SemEval task was to choose or classify relationships, rather than acquire and apply relationships. Additionally, the relationship classes they use are not necessarily within the scope of *common sense knowledge*.

Similar to our research, in (Agirre et al., 2001) knowledge is acquired about WordNet concepts. They find topics signatures, sets of related words, based on data from the Web and use them for word sense disambiguation. However, the type of relationship between words of a topic signature and the WordNet concept is not made explicit, and the authors find the topic signatures are not very effective for word sense disambiguation.

Finally, we note one approach to using the Web for NLP applications is to acquire knowledge on the fly. Previous work has approached solutions to word sense disambiguation by acquiring words or phrases directly based on the sentences or words being disambiguated (Martinez et al., 2006; Schwartz and Gomez, 2008). These methods dynamically acquire the data at runtime, rather than automatically create a common sense database of relations that is readily available. Additionally, in our current approach, we are able to acquire explicit *CSK* relationships.

3 Common Sense Acquisition

The two major phases of our framework, "Noun Acquisition" and "Concept Analysis", are outlined in Figure 1 and described within this section.

3.1 Noun Acquisition

The first step of our method is to acquire nouns (as words) from the Web which are in a relationship with other nouns. A Web search is performed in order to retrieve samples of text matching a *web query* created from a *search phrase* for the relationship. Each sample is syntactically parsed to verify a match with the corresponding *web query*, and the noun(s) filling a missing constituent of the parse are recorded.

The framework itself is very flexible, and it can handle the acquisition of words from other parts of speech. However, to be clear, we focus the explanation on the use of the framework to acquire specific types of relationships between nouns. Below we describe the procedures in more detail.

3.1.1 Creating Web Queries

Web queries are created semi-automatically by defining these parameters of a *search phrase*:

nounA the first noun phrase
nounB the second noun phrase
prep preposition, if any, used in the phrase
verb verb, if any, used in the phrase.

Table 2 lists all of the *search phrases* we use, one of which we use as an example throughout this section:

place *nounA prep nounB*

The verb, "place" in this case, is statically defined as part of the *search phrase*.

Prepositions were chosen to describe the type of relationship we were seeking to acquire as described in the background section. We limited ourselves to the "on" and "in" relationships since these were the most common.

on = (*on, onto, atop, upon, on top of, down on*)
in = (*in, into, inside, within, inside of*)

When noun parameters are provided, determiners or possessive pronouns selected from the list below are included. This provides greater accuracy in our search results.

det = (*the, a/an, this, that, my, your, his, her*)

Finally, the undefined parameters are replaced with a '*'. Below is a *web query* created from our *search phrase* where *nounB* is 'refrigerator', *prep* is 'in', *det* is 'the', and *nounA* is undefined:

place * in the refrigerator

3.1.2 Searching the Web

Given a *nounB*, The search algorithm can be summarized through the pseudocode below.

```
for each search_phrase
   for each prep
      for each det
         query = create_query(search_phrase,
                              prep, det, nounB));
         samples = websearch(query);
```

The searches were carried out through the Google Search API[2], or the Yahoo! Search Web Services[3]. Each *search phrase*, listed in Table 2, was run until a maximum of 2000 results were returned. Duplicate *samples* were removed to reduce the effects of websites replicating the text of one another.

[2]no longer supported by Google
[3]http://developer.yahoo.com/search/

relation	search phrase	voice
on, in	*nounA* is located *prep nounB* *nounA* is found *prep nounB* *nounA* is situated *prep nounB*	passive
on, in	*nounA* is *prep nounB* put *nounA prep nounB* place *nounA prep nounB* lay *nounA prep nounB* set *nounA prep nounB* locate *nounA prep nounB* position *nounA prep nounB*	active
on	hang *nounA prep nounB* mount *nounA prep nounB* attach *nounA prep nounB*	active

Table 2: *Search phrases* and relationships used for acquisition of *CSK*.

3.1.3 Parse and Match

The results we want to achieve in this step should describe a relationship:

nounA is [in | on] *nounB*

We use Charniak's parser (Charniak, 2000) on both the *web query* and the results returned from the web in order to ensure accuracy. To demonstrate this process, we extend our example, "place * in the refrigerator".

First, we get a parse with * (*nounA*) represented as 'something'.

(VP (VB place)
  (NP **(NN something)**)
  (PP (IN in) (NP (DT the) (NN refrigerator))))

We now know the constituent(s) which replace '(NN something)' will be our *nounA*. For example, in the following parse 'batter' is resolved as *nounA*.

(S1 (S (NP (PRP He))
  (VP (AUX was) (VP (VBN told) (S (VP (TO to)
    (VP (VB place)
      (NP (DT the) (JJ mixed) (NN batter))
      (PP (IN in) (NP (DT the) (NN refrigerator))))]

The head noun of the matching phrase is determined, which is 'batter' in the phrase '(DT the) (JJ mixed) (NN batter)'. Words are only recorded if they are present as a noun in WordNet. If the noun phrase contains a compound noun found in WordNet, then the compound noun is recorded instead.

The parse also helps to eliminate bad results. For the following sentence, the verb phrase does not match the parse of the *web query* due to an extra PP, and therefore we do not pull out "for several hours" as *nounA*.

```
(S1 (S (VP (VP (VB Mix)
          (NP (DT the) (NN sugar))
          (PRT (RP in))
          (PP (TO to) (NP (DT the) (NN dough))))
      (CC and)
      (VP (VB place)
          (PP (IN for) (NP (JJ several) (NNS hours)))
          (PP (IN in) (NP (DT the) (NN refrigerator)))))))
```

One may note that this malformed sentence is communicating that 'dough' is placed in the refrigerator, but the method does not handle this.

At the end of the noun acquisition phase, we are left with frequency counts of nouns being retrieved from a context matching the syntactic structure of a *web query*. This can easily be represented as the probability of a noun, *nA*, being returned to a query for the relationship, **R**, with noun *nB*.

$$p_w(nA, \mathbf{R}, nB)$$

This value along with the other steps we have gone over are stored in a MySQL relational database[4]. One could trace a relationship probability between nouns back to the web results which were matched to a *web query*, and even determine the abstract *search phrase* which produced the web query.

3.2 Concept Analysis

A focus of this work is on going beyond relationships between words. We would like to acquire knowledge about specific concepts in WordNet. In particular, we are trying to induce:

conceptA is [in | on] *nounB*.

where *conceptA* is a concept in WordNet (such as a sense of *nounA*), and *nounB* remains simply a word.

For the analysis, we rely on the vast amount of nouns we are able to acquire in order to create probabilities for relationships of *conceptA***R***nounB*. To get a grasp of the idea in general, consider 'table' as a *nounB* of interest. By examining all possible hypernyms of all senses of each $nounA$ one will find it is common for abstract entities to be "in a table" (i.e. data in a table), artifacts to be "on a table" (i.e. cup on a table), and physical things (including living things) to be "at a table" (i.e. the employees at the table). The same idea could be applied in reverse if one acquires knowledge for a set of *nounA*s. However, this paper only focuses on acquiring knowledge for the *nounB* constituent in a *search phrase*.

To begin with, one should note that concepts in WordNet are represented as synsets. A synset is a group of word-senses that have the same meaning. For example, *(batter-1, hitter-1, slugger-1, batsman-1)* is a synset with the meaning "(baseball) a ballplayer who is batting". We use WordNet version 3.0 in order to take advantage of the latest updates and corrections to the noun ontology. Since a word has multiple senses, we represent the probability that a word-sense, nAs, resulted from a query for a relationship, **R** with *nounB* as:

$$p_{ns}(nAs, \mathbf{R}, nB) = \frac{p_w(lemma(nAs), \mathbf{R}, nB)}{senses(lemma(nAs))}$$

where $senses$ returns the number of senses of the word $(lemma)$ within the word-sense nAs. We can then extend the probability to apply to a synset, $syns$, as:

$$p_{syn}(syns, \mathbf{R}, nB) = \sum_{nAs \in syns} p_{ns}(nAs, \mathbf{R}, nB)$$

Finally, we define a recursive function based on the idea that a concept subsumes all concepts below it (hyponyms) in the WordNet ontology:

$$P_c(cA, \mathbf{R}, nB) = p_{syn}(syns(cA), \mathbf{R}, nB) + \sum_{h \in hypos(cA)} P_c(h, \mathbf{R}, nB)$$

where cA is a concept/node in WordNet, $syns$ returns the synset which represents the concept, and $hypos$ returns the set of all direct hyponyms within the WordNet ontology. For example, *(money-3)* is a *(currency-1)*, so $P_c(\textit{currency-1}, \mathbf{R}, nB)$ receives $p_{syn}((\textit{money-3}), \mathbf{R}, nB)$ among others. This type of calculation over WordNet follows much like that of Resnik's (1999) *information-content* calculation. Note that the function no longer recurs when reaching a concept with no hyponyms and that $P_c(\textit{entity-1}, \mathbf{R}, nB)$ is always 1 (*entity-1* is the root node). P_c now represents a probability for the relationship: *conceptA***R***nounB*.

[4] http://www.mysql.com

nounB	***#nounAs***	***nounB***	***#nounAs***
basket	3300	boat	2787
bookcase	260	bottle	4742
bowl	5252	cabin	720
cabinet	1474	canoe	163
car	5534	ceiling	1187
city	1432	desk	4770
drawer	1638	dresser	698
floor	2850	house	4627
jar	4462	kitchen	2948
pocket	4771	refrigerator	2897
road	5493	room	5023
shelf	2581	ship	1469
sink	296	sofa	509
table	5312	truck	528
van	301	wall	2285

Table 3: List of nouns which fill the $nounB$ constituent in a *search phrase*, and the corresponding occurrences of $nounA$s acquired for each.

4 Evaluation

Our evaluation focuses on the applicability of the acquired *CSK*. We acquired relationships for the 30 nouns listed in Table 3. These nouns represent all possible words to fill the *nounB* constituent of a *search phrase*. The corresponding ***#nounAs*** indicates the number of *nounA*s that were acquired from the Web for each *nounB*. For example, 4771 *nounA*s were acquired for 'pocket'. This means 4771 results from the web matched the parse of a *web query* for 'pocket' and contained a *nounA* in WordNet (keeping in mind duplicates Web text were removed).

Delving deeper into our example, below are the top 20 *nounA*s found for the relationship *nounA***in***pocket*.

> *money, hand, cash, firework, something, dollar, ball, hands, key, coin, pedometer, card, battery, item, phone, penny, music, buck, implant, wallet*

As described in the concept analysis section, occurrences of each *nounA* for a given *nounB* lead to p_w values, which in turn are used to produce P_c values for concepts in WordNet. The application of *CSK* utilizes these probabilities rather than simply lists of words or even lists of concepts. However, challenges were encountered during the noun acquisition step before the probabilities were produced.

Many challenges of the noun acquisition step were overcome through the use of a parser. For example, phrases such as "Palestine is on the road to becoming..." could be eliminated since the parser marks the prepositional phrase "to becoming" as being attached to "the road". Thus, the parse of the web sample does not match the parse of the *web query* used to acquire it. Other times, noun-noun relationships were common simply because many web pages seem to copy the text of others. This problem was handled through the elimination of duplicate text samples from the Web. In the end, only about one in four results from the Web were actually used. Numbers in Table 3 reflect the result of these eliminations.

Some issues of the acquisition step were not directly addressed in this paper. A domain may tend to be more prevalent on the Internet and skew the *CSK*, such as *firework***in***pocket*. Another example, *baby***in***basket* was very common due to biblical references. Fictional works and metaphors also provided uncommon relationships dispersed within the results. Additionally, the parser makes mistakes. It was the hope that the *concept analysis* step would help to mitigate some noise from these problems. A final issue was the bottleneck of limited queries per day by the search engines, which restricted us to testing on only the 30 nouns listed.

4.1 Disambiguation System

The *CSK* is not intended to be used by itself for disambiguation. It would be far from accurate to assume the sense of a noun can be disambiguated simply by observing its relationship with one other noun in the sentence. For example, one of the test sentences incorporated the relationship *note***in***pocket*. Multiple senses of note are likely to be found in a pocket (i.e. the senses referring to "a brief written record", "a short personal letter", or "a piece of paper money"). In other cases, a relationship may not be found for any sense of a target word. Therefore, our knowledge is intended to be used as a reference, consulted by a disambiguation system.

We integrate our knowledge into a state of the art "all-words" word sense disambiguation algorithm. These algorithms are considered unsupervised or minimally supervised, because they do not require specific training data that is designed for instances of words in the testing data. In other words, these systems are designed to handle any word they come across. Our knowledge can supplement such a system, because the data can be acquired automatically for an unlimited number of nouns, assuming limitless web query restrictions.

The basis of our disambiguation system is the publicly available GWSD system (Sinha and Mihalcea, 2007). Sinha and Mihalcea report higher results on the Senseval-2 and Senseval-3 datasets than any of the participating unsupervised system. Additionally, GWSD is compatible with WordNet 3.0 and its output made it easy to integrate our knowledge. Sense predictions from four different graph metrics are produced, and we are able to incorporate our knowledge as another prediction within a voting scheme.

Considering the role of our knowledge as a reference, in some cases we would like the *CSK* to suggest multiple senses and in others none. For each target noun instance in the corpus, we lookup the $P_c(c, \mathbf{R}, nB)$ value, where c is the WordNet concept that corresponds to a sense of the target noun. We choose nB by matching the phrase "$in|on$ *det nB*" within the sentence. The system suggests all senses with a P_c value greater than 0.75 of the maximum P_c value over all senses. If no senses have a P_c value then no senses are suggested.

During voting, tallies of predictions and suggestions are taken for each sense of a noun. Ties are broken by choosing the lowest sense number among all those involved in the tie. Note that this is different than choosing the most frequent sense (i.e. the lowest sense number from *all* senses), in that only the top predicted senses are considered. This same type of voting is used with and without the *CSK* suggestions.

4.2 Experimental Corpus

A goal of our work was to acquire data which could be applied to NLP problems. We focus particularly on the difficult problem of *word sense disambiguation*. Due to the lack of sense tagged data, we were unable to find an annotated corpus with instances of all the nouns in Table 3 as prepositional complements. This was not surprising considering one of the reasons that minimally supervised approaches have become more popular is that they do not require hand-tagged training data (Mihalcea, 2002; Diab, 2004; McCarthy et al., 2004).

We created a corpus from sentences in Wikipedia which contained the phrase "$in|on$ *det lemma*", where *det* is a determiner or possessive pronoun, *lemma* is a noun from Table 3, and $in|on$ is a preposition for either relationship described earlier. Below we have provided an example from our corpus where the knowledge from 'pocket' can be applied to disambiguate 'key'.

> *Now Tony's* ***key*** *to the flat is in the pocket of his raincoat, so on returning to his flat some time later he realizes that he cannot get inside.*

The corpus[5] contained a total of 342 sentences, with one target noun annotated per sentence. The target nouns were selected to potentially fill the *nounA* constituent in the relationship *nounA***R***nounB*, and they were assigned all appropriate WordNet 3.0 senses. Considering the fine-grained nature of WordNet (Ide and Wilks, 2006), 26.3% of the instances were annotated with multiple senses. We also restricted the corpus to only include polysemous nouns, or nouns which had an additional sense beyond the senses assigned to it.

Inter-annotator agreement was used to validate the corpus. Because the corpus was built by an author of the work, we asked a non-author to re-annotate the corpus without knowledge of the original annotations. This second annotator was told to choose all appropriate senses just as did the original annotator. Agreement was calculated as:

$$\mathbf{agree} = \left(\sum_{i \in C} \frac{|S1_i \cap S2_i|}{|S1_i \cup S2_i|} \right) \div 342$$

where $S1$ and $S2$ are the two sets of sense annotations, and i is an instance of the corpus, C.

The agreement and other data concerning corpus annotation can be found in Table 4. As a point of comparison, the Senseval 3 all-words task had a 75% agreement on nouns (Snyder and Palmer, 2004). A second evaluation of agreement was also done. The non-author annotations were treated as if they came

[5]available at: http://eecs.ucf.edu/~hschwartz/CSK/

	insts	agree	$\mathbf{F1}_h$	$\mathbf{F1}_{rnd}$	$\mathbf{F1}_{MFS}$
on	131	79.9	84.7	28.2	71.0
in	211	80.8	91.9	27.2	67.8
both	342	80.5	89.2	27.6	69.0

Table 4: Experimental corpus data for each relationship (***on, in***). **insts**: number of annotated instances; **agree**: inter-annotator agreement %; **F1** values (precision = recall): h: human annotation, rnd: random baseline, MFS: most frequent sense baseline.

	without *CSK*		with *CSK*	
	$\mathbf{F1}_{all}$	$\mathbf{F1}_{indeg}$	$\mathbf{F1}_{all}$	$\mathbf{F1}_{indeg}$
on	62.6	63.4	64.9	67.2
in	68.7	69.7	71.6	72.5
both	66.4	**67.3**	69.0	**70.5**
ties	37	0	66	72

Table 5: F1 values (precision = recall) on our experimental corpus with and without *CSK*. $\mathbf{F1}_{all}$: using all 4 graph metrics; $\mathbf{F1}_{indeg}$: using only the indegree metric; **ties**: number of instances where tie votes occurred.

from a disambiguation system in order to get a human upper-bound of performance. Just as the automatic system handled tie votes, when one word had multiple sense annotations, the annotation with the lowest sense number was used. This performance upper-bound is shown as $\mathbf{F1}_h$ in Table 4.

4.3 Results

Our disambiguation results are presented in Table 5. We found that, in all cases, including *CSK* improved results. It turned out that 54.7% of the noun instances received at least one suggestion from the *CSK*, and 24.5% of the instances received multiple suggestions. It is not clear why the ***on*** results were slightly below that for ***in***. We suspect the ***on*** portion of the corpus was slightly more difficult because the human annotation ($\mathbf{F1}_h$) found a similar phenomenon.

One observation we made when setting up the test was that the indegree metric alone performed slightly better than using the votes of all four metrics. This was not surprising considering Sinha and Mihalcea found the indegree metric by itself to perform only slightly below a combination of metrics on the senseval data (Sinha and Mihalcea, 2007). Therefore, Table 5 also reports the use of the indegree metric by itself or with *CSK*, F1_{indeg}. In these cases we saw the greatest improvements of using *CSK*, producing an an error reduction of about 4.5% and outperforming the F1_{MFS} value.

Several additional experiments were performed. Note that even during ties, the chosen sense was taken from the predictions and suggestions. When we instead incorporated an MFS backoff strategy for ties, our top results for $\mathbf{F1}_{indeg}$ with *CSK* dropped to 70.2. We also ran a precision test with no predictions made for tie votes, and found a precision of 71.9% on the 270 instances that did not have a tie for top votes (this also used the indegree metric with *CSK*). All results supported our goal of acquiring *CSK* that was applicable to word sense disambiguation.

5 Conclusion

We found our acquired *CSK* to be useful when incorporated into a word sense disambiguation system, finding an error reduction of around 4.5% for top results. Relationships between nouns were acquired from the Web through a unique search method of filling constituents in a *search phrase*. Samples returned from the Web were restricted by a requirement to match the syntactic parse of a *web query*. The resulting data was analyzed over WordNet to produce probabilities of relationships in the form of *conceptA***R***nounB*, where *conceptA* is a concept in WordNet rather than an ambiguous noun.

In our effort to validate the knowledge through application, many steps along the way were left open for future investigations. First, there is a need to exhaustively search for *CSK* of all nouns and to acquire other forms of *CSK*. With this improvement *CSK* could be tested on a standard corpus, rather than a corpus focused on select nouns and prepositional phrases. Looking into acquisition improvements, a study of the effectiveness of the parse would be beneficial. Finally, the applicability of the knowledge may be increased through a more complex concept analysis or utilizing a more advanced voting scheme.

6 Acknowledgement

This research was supported by the NASA Engineering and Safety Center under Grant/Cooperative Agreement NNX08AJ98A.

References

Eneko Agirre, Olatz Ansa, and David Martinez. 2001. Enriching wordnet concepts with topic signatures. In *In Proceedings of the NAACL workshop on WordNet and Other Lexical Resources: Applications, Extensions and Customizations*, Pittsburg, USA.

Eugene Charniak. 2000. A maximum-entropy-inspired parser. In *Proceedings of the first conference on North American chapter of the Association for Computational Linguistics*, pages 132–139, San Francisco, CA, USA. Morgan Kaufmann Publishers Inc.

Timothy Chklovski and Patrick Pantel. 2004. Verbocean: Mining the web for fine-grained semantic verb relations. In *Proceedings of Conference on Empirical Methods in Natural Language Processing (EMNLP-04)*, Barcelona, Spain.

Mona Diab. 2004. Relieving the data acquisition bottleneck in word sense disambiguation. In *Proceedings of the 42nd Annual Meeting of the Association for Computational Linguistics (ACL'04)*, pages 303–310.

Roxana Girju, Preslav Nakov, Vivi Nastase, Stan Szpakowicz, Peter Turney, and Deniz Yuret. 2007. Semeval-2007 task 04: Classification of semantic relations between nominals. In *Proceedings of SemEval-2007*, pages 13–18, Prague, Czech Republic, June. Association for Computational Linguistics.

Marti A. Hearst. 1992. Automatic acquisition of hyponyms from large text corpora. In *In Proceedings of the 14th International Conference on Computational Linguistics (COLING-92)*, pages 539–545.

Nancy Ide and Yorick Wilks, 2006. *Word Sense Disambiguation: Algorithms And Applications*, chapter 3: Making Sense About Sense. Springer.

Douglas B. Lenat. 1995. CYC: a large-scale investment in knowledge infrastructure. *Communications of the ACM*, 38(11):33–38.

H. Liu and P Singh. 2004. Conceptnet: A practical commonsense reasoning toolkit. *BT Technology Journal*, 22:211–226.

David Martinez, Eneko Agirre, and Xinglong Wang. 2006. Word relatives in context for word sense disambiguation. In *Proceedings of the 2006 Australasian Language Technology Workshop*, pages 42–50.

Diana McCarthy, Rob Koeling, Julie Weeds, and John Carroll. 2004. Finding predominant word senses in untagged text. In *Proceedings of the 42nd Meeting of the Association for Computational Linguistics*, pages 279–286, Barcelona, Spain, July. Association for Computational Linguistics.

Rada Mihalcea. 2002. Bootstrapping large sense tagged corpora. In *Proceedings of the 3rd International Conference on Languages Resources and Evaluations LREC 2002*, Las Palmas, Spain, May.

George Miller, R. Beckwith, Christiane Fellbaum, D. Gross, and K. Miller. 1993. Five papers on wordnet. Technical report, Princeton University.

Kathy Panton, Cynthia Matuszek, Douglas Lenat, Dave Schneider, Michael Witbrock, Nick Siegel, and Blake Shepard. 2006. Common sense reasoning : From cyc to intelligent assistant. In Y. Cai and J. Abascal, editors, *Ambient Intelligence in Everyday Life*, pages 1–31.

Randolph Quirk, Sidney Greenbaum, Geoffrey Leech, and Jan Svartvik. 1985. *A Comprehensive Grammaer of the English Language*. Longman.

Philip Resnik. 1999. Semantic similarity in a taxonomy: An information-based measure and its application to problems of ambiguity in natural language. *Journal of Artificial Intelligence Research*, 11:95–130.

Hansen A. Schwartz and Fernando Gomez. 2008. Acquiring knowledge from the web to be used as selectors for noun sense disambiguation. In *CoNLL 2008: Proceedings of the Twelfth Conference on Computational Natural Language Learning*, pages 105–112, Manchester, England, August.

Ravi Sinha and Rada Mihalcea. 2007. Unsupervised graph-based word sense disambiguation using measures of word semantic similarity. Irvine, CA, September.

Benjamin Snyder and Martha Palmer. 2004. The English all-words task. In *ACL Senseval-3 Workshop*, Barcelona, Spain, July.

Utilizing Contextually Relevant Terms in Bilingual Lexicon Extraction

Azniah Ismail
Department of Computer Science
University of York
York YO10 5DD UK
azniah@cs.york.ac.uk

Suresh Manandhar
Department of Computer Science
University of York
York YO10 5DD UK
suresh@cs.york.ac.uk

Abstract

This paper demonstrates one efficient technique in extracting bilingual word pairs from non-parallel but comparable corpora. Instead of using the common approach of taking high frequency words to build up the initial bilingual lexicon, we show contextually relevant terms that co-occur with cognate pairs can be efficiently utilized to build a bilingual dictionary. The result shows that our models using this technique have significant improvement over baseline models especially when highest-ranked translation candidate per word is considered.

1 Introduction

Bilingual lexicons or dictionaries are invaluable knowledge resources for language processing tasks. The compilation of such bilingual lexicons remains as a substantial issue to linguistic fields. In general practice, many linguists and translators spend huge amounts of money and effort to compile this type of knowledge resources either manually, semi-automatically or automatically. Thus, obtaining the data is expensive.

In this paper, we demonstrate a technique that utilizes contextually relevant terms that co-occur with cognate pairs to expand an initial bilingual lexicon. We use unannotated resources that are freely available such as English-Spanish Europarl corpus (Koehn, 2005) and another different set of cognate pairs as seed words.

We show that this technique is able to achieve high precision score for bilingual lexicon extracted from non-parallel but comparable corpora. Our model using this technique with spelling similarity approach obtains 85.4 percent precision at 50.0 percent recall. Precision of 79.0 percent at 50.0 percent recall is recorded when using this technique with context similarity approach. Furthermore, by using a string edit-distance vs. precision curve, we also reveal that the latter model is able to capture words efficiently compared to a baseline model.

Section 2 is dedicated to mention some of the related works. In Section 3, the technique that we used is explained. Section 4 describes our experimental setup followed by the evaluation results in Section 5. Discussion and conclusion are in Section 6 and 7 respectively.

2 Related Work

Koehn and Knight (2002) describe few potential clues that may help in extracting bilingual lexicon from two monolingual corpora such as identical words, similar spelling, and similar context features. In reporting our work, we treat both identical word pairs and similar spelling word pairs as *cognate pairs*.

Koehn and Knight (2002) map 976 identical word pairs that are found in their two monolingual German-English corpora and report that 88.0 percent of them are correct. They propose to restrict the word length, at least of length 6, to increase the accuracy of the collected word pairs. Koehn and Knight (2002) mention few related works that use different measurement to compute the similarity, such as longest common subsequence ratio (Melamed, 1995) and string edit distance (Mann

Proceedings of the NAACL HLT Workshop on Unsupervised and Minimally Supervised Learning of Lexical Semantics, pages 10–17,
Boulder, Colorado, June 2009.

and Yarowski, 2001). However, Koehn and Knight (2002) point out that majority of their word pairs do not show much resemblance at all since they use German-English language pair. Haghighi et al. (2008) mention one disadvantage of using edit distance, that is, precision quickly degrades with higher recall. Instead, they propose assigning a feature to each substring of length of three or less for each word.

For approaches based on contextual features or context similarity, we assume that for a word that occurs in a certain context, its translation equivalent also occurs in equivalent contexts. Contextual features are the frequency counts of context words occurring in the surrounding of target word *W*. A context vector for each *W* is then constructed, with only context words found in the seed lexicon. The context vectors are then translated into the target language before their similarity is measured.

Fung and Yee (1998) point out that not only the number of common words in context gives some similarity clue to a word and its translation, but the actual ranking of the context word frequencies also provides important clue to the similarity between a bilingual word pair. This fact has motivated Fung and Yee (1998) to use *tfidf* weighting to compute the vectors. This idea is similar to Rapp (1999) who proposed to transform all co-occurrence vectors using *log likelihood ratio* instead of just using the frequency counts of the co-occurrences. These values are used to define whether the context words are highly associated with the *W* or not.

Earlier work relies on a large bilingual dictionary as their seed lexicon (Rapp, 1999; Fung and Yee, 1998; among others). Koehn and Knight (2002) present one interesting idea of using extracted cognate pairs from corpus as the seed words in order to alleviate the need of huge, initial bilingual lexicon. Haghighi et al. (2008), amongst a few others, propose using canonical correlation analysis to reduce the dimension. Haghighi et al (2008) only use a small-sized bilingual lexicon containing 100 word pairs as seed lexicon. They obtain 89.0 percent precision at 33.0 percent recall for their English-Spanish induction with best feature set, using topically similar but non-parallel corpora.

3 The Utilizing Technique

Most works in bilingual lexicon extraction use lists of high frequency words that are obtained from source and target language corpus to be their source and target word lists respectively. In our work, we aim to extract a high precision bilingual lexicon using different approach. Instead, we use list of contextually relevant terms that co-occur with cognate pairs.

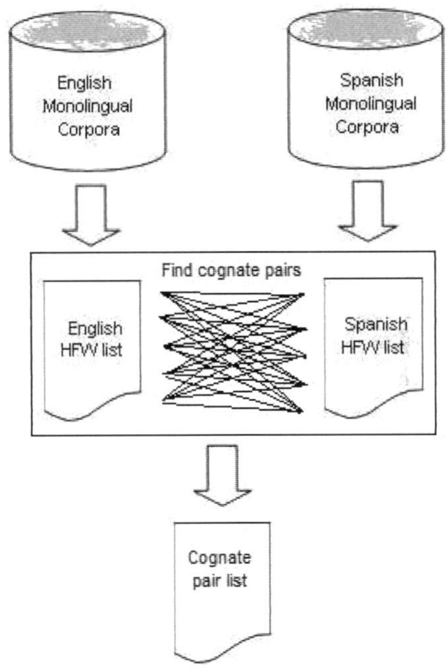

Figure 1: Cognate pair extraction

These cognate pairs can be derived automatically by mapping or finding identical words occur in two high frequency list of two monolingual corpora (see Figure 1). They are used to acquire list of source word W_s and target word W_t. W_s and W_t are contextually relevant terms that highly co-occur with the cognate pairs in the same context. Thus, log likelihood measure can be used to identify them.

Next, bilingual word pairs are extracted among words in these W_s and W_t list using either context similarity or spelling similarity. Figure 2 shows some examples of potential bilingual word pairs, of W_s and W_t, co-occurring with identical cognate pairs of word *'civil'*.

As we are working on English-Spanish language pair, we extract bilingual lexicon using string edit distance to identify spelling similarity between W_s

and W_t. Figure 3 outlines the algorithm using spelling similarity in more detail.

Using the same W_s and W_t lists, we extract bilingual lexicon by computing the context similarity between each $\{W_s, W_t\}$ pair. To identify the context similarity, the relation between each $\{W_s, W_t\}$ pair can be detected automatically using a vector similarity measure such as *cosine measure* as in (1). The A and B are the elements in the context vectors, containing either zero or non-zero seed word values for W_s and W_t, respectively.

$$Cosine \text{ similarity} = cos(\theta) = \frac{A \times B}{||A|| \times ||B||} \quad (1)$$

The cosine measure favors $\{W_s, W_t\}$ pairs that share the most number of non-zero seed word values. However, one disadvantage of this measure is that the cosine value directly proportional to the actual W_s and W_t values. Even though W_s and W_t might not closely correlated with the same set of seed words, the matching score could be high if W_s or W_t has high seed word values everywhere. Thus, we transform the context vectors from real value into binary vectors before the similarity is computed. Figure 4 outlines the algorithm using context similarity in more detail.

In the algorithm, after the W_s and W_t lists are obtained, each W_s and W_t units is represented by their context vector containing log likelihood (LL) values of contextually relevant words, occurring in the seed lexicon, that highly co-occur with the W_s and W_t respectively. To get this context vector, for each W_s and W_t, all sentences in the English or Spanish corpora containing the respective word are extracted to form a particular sub corpus, e.g. sub corpus *society* is a collection of sentences containing the source word *society*.

Using window size of a sentence, the LL value of term occurring with the word W_s or W_t in their respective sub corpora is computed. Term that is highly associated with the W_s or W_t is called contextually relevant term. However, we consider each term with LL value higher than certain threshold (e.g. *threshold* $\geq$ 15.0) to be contextually relevant. Contextually relevant terms occurring in the seed lexicon are used to build the context vector for the

CIVIL	
society	sociedad
rights	derechos
development	desarrollo
cooperation	cooperación
military	militar
dialogue	diálogo
representatives	representantes
democracy	democracia
international	internacional
forces	fuerzas
government	gobierno
security	seguridad
participation	participación
conflict	conflicto
freedoms	libertades
aviation	aviación
protection	protección
organisations	organizaciónes
organisation	organización
administration	administración

Figure 2: Bilingual word pairs are found within context of cognate word *civil*

1. Automatic cognate pairs derivation
Obtain high frequency lists from both monolingual corpora => HFW_S and HFW_T lists.
For all pairs taken from the HFW_S and HFW_T lists, find identical cognate pairs, C.

2. Source word and target word list
For every C :
Extract all sentences containing C =>*Sub corpora C*
Using window size of a sentence for *Sub corpora C*, compute the log likelihood of all terms occurring with word C => LL_C
From LL_C, obtain 100 highly-ranked contextually relevant terms in respective language => W_s and W_t

3. Spelling similarity measure
For every pair of W_s and W_t :
Compute similarity using edit distance => *SpellingSim*(W_s, W_t)
Obtain all matched bilingual word pairs above threshold or highest-ranked word pairs.

Figure 3: Utilizing technique with spelling similarity

1. Automatic cognate pairs derivation

Obtain high frequency lists from both monolingual corpora => HFW_S and HFW_T lists.

For all pairs taken from the HFW_S and HFW_T lists, find identical cognate pairs, C.

2. Source word and target word list

For every C :

Extract all sentences containing C => *Sub corpora C*

Using window size of a sentence for *Sub corpora C* , compute the log likelihood of all terms occurring with word C => LL_C

From LL_C, obtain 100 highly-ranked contextually relevant terms in respective language => W_s and W_t

3. Context term extraction

For every W_s and W_t :

Extract all sentences containing the word respectively => *Sub corpora* W_s and *Sub corpora* W_t

Using window size of a sentence, compute the log-likelihood of all terms occurring with word W_s and W_t => LL_s and LL_t

Obtain high ranked contextually relevant terms above certain threshold => CT_s and CT_t

4. Context vector builder

For every W_s and W_t:

Obtain only CT_s and CT_t that are found in seed word to form real valued context vector => RCV_s and RCV_t .

Transform the values into binary context vector => $BitCV_s$ and $BitCV_t$

5. Context Similarity Measure

For every pair of W_s and W_t:

Compute similarity using $BitCV_s$ and $BitCV_t$ => *ContextSim* (W_s, W_t)

Obtain all matched bilingual word pairs above threshold or highest-ranked word pairs.

Figure 4: Utilizing technique with context similarity

W_s or W_t respectively. For example, word *participation* and *education* occurring in the seed lexicon are contextually relevant terms for source word *society*. Thus, they become elements of the context vector. Then, we transform the context vectors, from real value into binary, before we compute the similarity with cosine measure.

4 Experimental Setup

4.1 Data

For source and target monolingual corpus, we derive English and Spanish sentences from parallel Europarl corpora (Koehn, 2005).

- We split each of them into three parts; year 1996 - 1999, year 2000 - 2003 and year 2004 - 2006.
- We only take the first part, about 400k sentences of Europarl Spanish (year 1996 - 1999) and 2nd part, also about 400k from Europarl English (year 2000 - 2003). We refer the particular part taken from the source language corpus as S and the other part of the target language corpus as T.

This approach is quite common in order to obtain non-parallel but comparable (or same domain) corpus. Examples can be found in Fung and Cheung (2004), followed by Haghighi et al. (2008). For corpus pre-processing, we only use sentence boundary detection and tokenization on raw text. We decided that large quantities of raw text requiring minimum processing could also be considered as minimal since they are inexpensive and not limited. These should contribute to low or medium density languages for which annotated resources are limited. We also clean all tags and filter out stop words from the corpus.

4.2 Evaluation

We extracted our evaluation lexicon from *Word Reference** free online dictionary . For this work, the word types are not restricted but mostly are content words. We have two sets of evaluation. In one, we take high ranked candidate pairs where W_s could have multiple translations. In the other, we only consider highest-ranked W_t for each W_s. For evaluation purposes, we take only the top 2000 candidate ranked-pairs from the output. From that list, only candidate pairs with words found in the evaluation lexicon are proposed. We use F1-measure to evaluate proposed lexicon against the evaluation lexicon. The recall is defined as the proportion of the high ranked candidate pairs. The precision is given as the number of correct candidate pairs divided by the total number of proposed candidate pairs.

4.3 Other Setups

The following were also setup and used:

- *List of cognate pairs*
  We obtained 79 identical cognate pairs from the

*from website `http://www.wordreference.com`

top 2000 high frequency lists of our *S* and *T* but we chose 55 of these that have at least 100 contextually relevant terms that are highly associated with each of them.

- *Seed lexicon*
We also take a set of cognate pairs to be our seed lexicon. We defined the size of a small seed lexicon ranges between 100 to 1k word pairs. Hence, our seed lexicon containing 700 cognate pairs are still considered as a small-sized seed lexicon. However, instead of acquiring this set of cognate pairs automatically, we compiled the cognate pairs from a few *Learning Spanish Cognates* websites [†]. This approach is a simple alternative to replace the 10-20k general dictionaries (Rapp, 1999; Fung and McKeown, 2004) or automatic seed words (Koehn and Knight, 2002; Haghighi et al., 2008). However, this approach can only be used if the source and target language are fairly related and both share lexically similar words that most likely have same meaning. Otherwise, we have to rely on general bilingual dictionaries.

- *Stop list*
Previously (Rapp, 1999; Koehn and Knight, 2002; among others) suggested filtering out commonly occurring words that do not help in processing natural language data. This idea sometimes seem as a negative approach to the natural articles of language, however various studies have proven that it is sensible to do so.

- *Baseline system*
We build baseline systems using basic context similarity and spelling similarity features.

5 Evaluation Results

For the first evaluation, candidate pairs are ranked after being measured either with cosine for context similarity or edit distance for spelling similarity. In this evaluation, we take the first 2000 of $\{W_s, W_t\}$ candidate pairs from the proposed lexicon where W_s may have multiple translations or multiple W_t. See Table 1.

[†]such as http://www.colorincolorado.org and http://www.language-learning-advisor.com

Setting	$P_{0.1}$	$P_{0.25}$	$P_{0.33}$	$P_{0.5}$	Best-F1
ContextSim (*CS*)	42.9	69.6	60.7	58.7	49.6
SpellingSim (*SS*)	90.5	74.2	69.9	64.6	50.9

(a) from baseline models

Setting	$P_{0.1}$	$P_{0.25}$	$P_{0.33}$	$P_{0.5}$	Best-F1
E-ContextSim (*ECS*)	78.3	73.5	71.8	64.0	51.2
E-SpellingSim (*ESS*)	95.8	75.6	71.8	63.4	51.5

(b) from our proposed models

Table 1: Performance of baseline and our model for top 2000 candidates below certain threshold and ranked

Setting	$P_{0.1}$	$P_{0.25}$	$P_{0.33}$	$P_{0.5}$	Best-F1
ContextSim-Top1 (*CST*)	58.3	61.2	64.8	55.2	52.6
SpellingSim-Top1 (*SST*)	84.9	66.4	52.7	34.5	37.0

(a) from baseline models

Setting	$P_{0.1}$	$P_{0.25}$	$P_{0.33}$	$P_{0.5}$	Best-F1
E-ContextSim-Top1 (*ECST*)	85.0	81.1	79.7	79.0	57.1
E-SpellingSim-Top1 (*ESST*)	100.0	93.6	91.6	85.4	59.0

(b) from our proposed models

Table 2: Performance of baseline and our model for top 2000 candidates of top 1

Using either context or spelling similarity approach on *S* and *T* (labeled *ECS* and *ESS* respectively), our models achieved about 51.2 percent of best F1 measure. Those are not a significant improvement with only 1.0 to 2.0 percent error reduction over the baseline models (labeled *CS* and *SS*).

For the second evaluation, we take the first 2000 of $\{W_s, W_t\}$ pairs where W_s may only have the highest ranked W_t as translation candidates (See Table 2). This time, both of our models (with context similarity and spelling similarity, labeled *ECST* and *ESST* respectively) yielded almost 60.0 percent of best F1 measure. It is noted that using *ESST* alone recorded a significant improvement of 20.0 percent in the F1 score compared to *SST* baseline model. *ESST* obtained 85.4 percent precision at 50.0 percent recall. Precision of 79.0 percent at 50.0 percent recall is recorded when using *ECST*. However, the *ECST* has not recorded a significant difference over *CST* baseline model (57.1 and 52.6 percent respectively) in the second evaluation. The overall performances, represented by precision scores for different

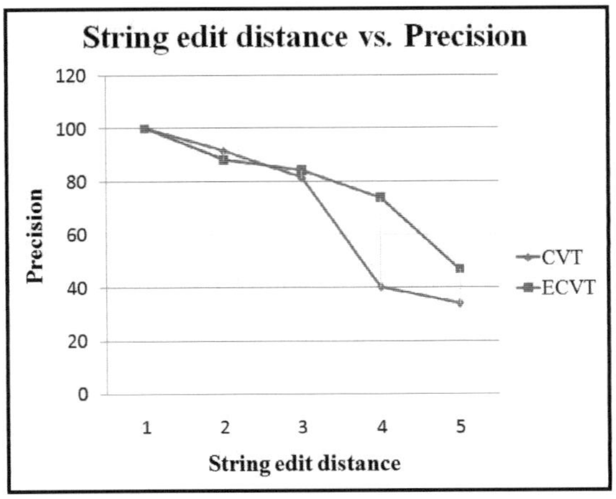

Figure 5: String Edit Distance vs. Precision curve

range of recalls, for these four models are illustrated in *Appendix A*.

It is important to see the inner performance of the *ECST* model with further analysis. We present a string edit distance value (*EDv*) vs. precision curve for *ECST* and *CST* in Figure 5 to measure the performance of the *ECST* model in capturing bilingual pairs with less similar orthographic features, those that may not be captured using spelling similarity.

The graph in Figure 5 shows that even though *CST* has higher precision score than *ECST* at *EDv* of 2, it is not significant (the difference is less than 5.0 percent) and the spelling is still similar. On the other hand, precision for proposed lexicon with *EDv* above 3 (where the W_s and the proposed translation equivalent W_t spelling becoming more dissimilar) using *ECST* is higher than *CST*. The most significant difference of the precision is almost 35.0 percent, where *ECST* achieved almost 75.0 percent precision compared to *CST* with 40.0 percent precision at *EDv* of 4. It is followed by *ECST* with almost 50.0 percent precision compared to *CST* with precision less than 35.0 percent, offering about 15.0 percent precision improvement at *EDv* of 5.

6 Discussion

As we are working on English-Spanish language pair, we could have focused on spelling similarity feature only. Performance of the model using this feature usually record higher accuracy otherwise they may not be commonly occurring in a corpus. Our models with this particular feature have recorded higher F1 scores especially when considering only the highest-ranked candidates.

We also experiment with context similarity approach. We would like to see how far this approach helps to add to the candidate scores from our corpus *S* and *T*. The other reason is sometimes a correct target is not always a cognate even though a cognate for it is available. Our *ECST* model has not recorded significant improvement over *CST* baseline model in the F1-measure. However, we were able to show that by utilizing contextually relevant terms, *ECST* gathers more correct candidate pairs especially when it comes to words with dissimilar spelling. This means that *ECST* is able to add more to the candidate scores compared to *CST*. Thus, more correct translation pairs can be expected with a good combination of *ECST* and *ESST*.

The following are the advantages of our utilizing technique:

- Reduced errors, hence able to improve precision scores.
- Extraction is more efficient in the contextual boundaries (see Appendix B for examples).
- Context similarity approach within our technique has a potential to add more to the candidate scores.

Yet, our attempt using cognate pairs as seed words is more appropriate for language pairs that share large number of cognates or similar spelling words with same meaning. Otherwise, one may have to rely on bilingual dictionaries.

There may be some possible supporting strategies, which we could use to help improve further the precision score within the utilizing technique. For example, dimension reduction using canonical correlation analysis (CCA), resemblance detection, measure of dispersion, reference corpus and further noise reduction. However, we do not include a reranking method, as we are using collection of cognate pairs instead of a general bilingual dictionary. Since our corpus *S* and *T* is in similar domain, we might still not have seen the potential of this technique in its entirety. One may want to test the technique with different type of corpora for future works.

Nevertheless, we are still concerned that many spurious translation equivalents were proposed because the words actually have higher correlation with the input source word compared to the real target word. Otherwise, the translation equivalents may not be in the boundaries or in the corpus from which translation equivalents are to be extracted. Haghighi et al (2008) have reported that the most common errors detected in their analysis on top 100 errors were from semantically related words, which had strong context feature correlations. Thus, the issue remains. We leave all these for further discussion in future works.

7 Conclusion

We present a bilingual lexicon extraction technique that utilizes contextually relevant terms that co-occur with cognate pairs to expand an initial bilingual lexicon. We show that this utilizing technique is able to achieve high precision score for bilingual lexicon extracted from non-parallel but comparable corpora. We demonstrate this technique using unannotated resources that are freely available.

Our model using this technique with spelling similarity obtains 85.4 percent precision at 50.0 percent recall. Precision of 79.0 percent at 50.0 percent recall is recorded when using this technique with context similarity approach. We also reveal that the latter model with context similarity is able to capture words efficiently compared to a baseline model. Thus, we show contextually relevant terms that co-occur with cognate pairs can be efficiently utilized to build a bilingual dictionary.

References

Cranias, L., Papageorgiou, H, and Piperidis, S. 1994. A matching technique in Example-Based Machine Translation. *In International Conference On Computational Linguistics Proceedings*, 15th conference on Computational linguistics, Kyoto, Japan.

Diab, M., and Finch, S. 2000. A statistical word-level translation model for comparable corpora. *In Proceedings of the Conference on Content-based multimedia information access (RIAO)*.

Fung, P., and Cheung, P. 2004. Mining very non-parallel corpora: Parallel sentence and lexicon extraction via bootstrapping and EM. *In Proceedings of the 2004 Conference on Empirical Method in Natural Language Processing (EMNLP)*, Barcelona, Spain.

Fung, P., and Yee, L.Y. 1998. An IR Approach for Translating New Words from Nonparallel, Comparable Texts. *In Proceedings of COLING-ACL98*, Montreal, Canada, 1998.

Fung, P., and McKeown, K. 1997. Finding Terminology Translations from Non-parallel Corpora. *In The 5th Annual Workshop on Very Large Corpora*, Hong Kong, Aug 1997.

Haghighi, A., Liang, P., Berg-Krikpatrick, T., and Klein, D. 2008. Learning bilingual lexicons from monolingual corpora. *In Proceedings of The ACL 2008*, June 15 -20 2008, Columbus, Ohio

Koehn, P. 2005. Europarl: a parallel corpus for statistical machine translation. *In MT Summit*

Koehn, P., and Knight , K. 2001. Knowledge sources for word-level translation models. *In Proceedings of the Conference on Empirical Methods in Natural Language Processing (EMNLP)*.

Koehn, P., and Knight , K. 2002. Learning a translation lexicon from monolingual corpora. *In Proceedings of ACL 2002*, July 2002, Philadelphia, USA, pp. 9-16.

Rapp, R. 1995. Identifying word translations in non-parallel texts. *In Proceedings of ACL 33*, pages 320-322.

Rapp, R. 1999. Automatic identification of word translations from unrelated English and German corpora. *In Proceedings of ACL 37*, pages 519-526.

Appendix A. Precision scores with different recalls

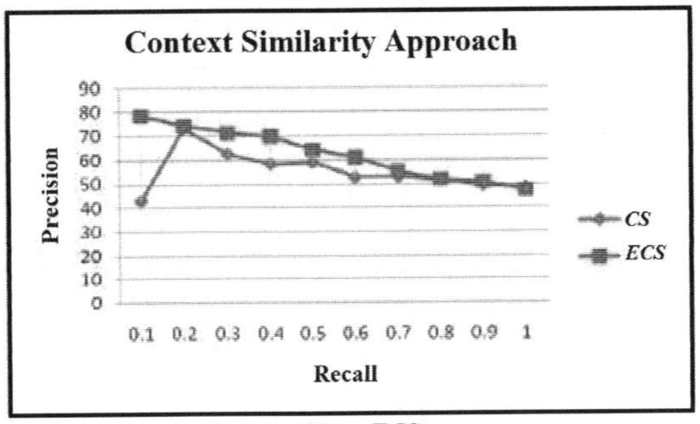

CS vs. ECS

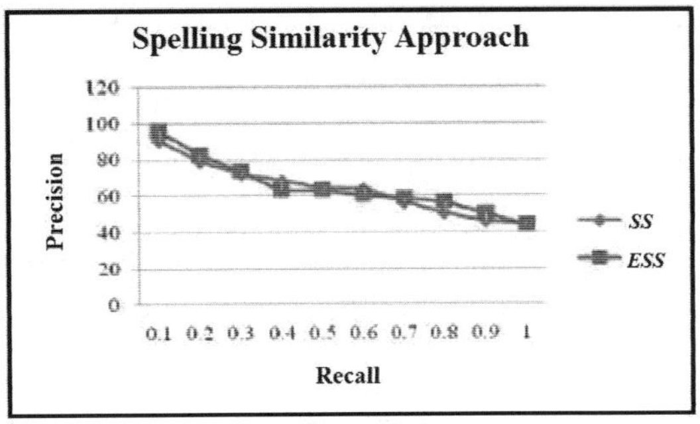

SS vs. ESS

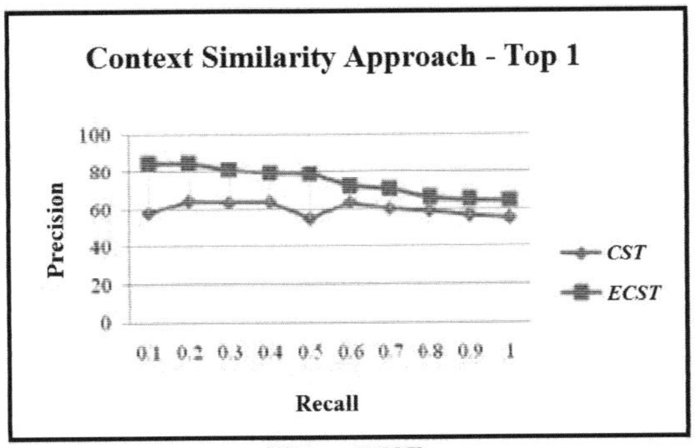

CST vs. ECST

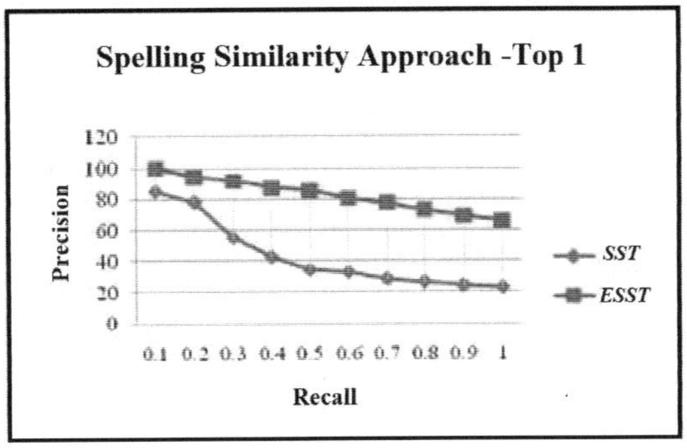

SST vs. ESST

Appendix B. Some examples of effective extraction via utilizing technique

Source	Target	ECVT		CV		Rank
		Candidate found	Sim. value	Candidate found	Sim. value	
clause	*clausula*	***clausula***	***0.402015126***	*autentica* *fortalecimiento* *economico* *respeto* *vigor* ***clausula***	*0.447213595* *0.430331483* *0.412478956* *0.40824829* *0.402015126* ***0.402015126***	1 2 < > < > < > < >
pillar	*pilar*	***pilar***	***0.547722558***	*daramente* ***pilar*** *basada* *comercial* *iniciado* *exterior* *agricola*	*0.632455532* ***0.547722558*** *0.53935989* *0.516397779* *0.516397779* *0.478091444* *0.447213595*	1 2 3 4 4 5 6
state	*estado*	***estado***	***0.433012702***	*derecho* ***estado*** *respeto*	*0.43519414* ***0.433012702*** *0.412478956*	1 2 < >
confidence	*confianza*	***confianza***	***0.424264069***	*errores* *desarrollo* *haberse* *demuestran* *deficiencias* ***confianza***	*0.447213595* *0.447213595* *0.447213595* *0.447213595* *0.447213595* ***0.424264069***	1 1 1 1 1 2
welfare	*bienestar*	***bienestar***	***0.40824829***	*hubiera* ***bienestar***	*0.500000000* ***0.40824829***	1 < >

Corpus-based Semantic Lexicon Induction with Web-based Corroboration

Sean P. Igo
Center for High Performance Computing
University of Utah
Salt Lake City, UT 84112 USA
Sean.Igo@utah.edu

Ellen Riloff
School of Computing
University of Utah
Salt Lake City, UT 84112 USA
riloff@cs.utah.edu

Abstract

Various techniques have been developed to automatically induce semantic dictionaries from text corpora and from the Web. Our research combines corpus-based semantic lexicon induction with statistics acquired from the Web to improve the accuracy of automatically acquired domain-specific dictionaries. We use a weakly supervised bootstrapping algorithm to induce a semantic lexicon from a text corpus, and then issue Web queries to generate co-occurrence statistics between each lexicon entry and semantically related terms. The Web statistics provide a source of independent evidence to confirm, or disconfirm, that a word belongs to the intended semantic category. We evaluate this approach on 7 semantic categories representing two domains. Our results show that the Web statistics dramatically improve the ranking of lexicon entries, and can also be used to filter incorrect entries.

1 Introduction

Semantic resources are extremely valuable for many natural language processing (NLP) tasks, as evidenced by the wide popularity of WordNet (Miller, 1990) and a multitude of efforts to create similar "WordNets" for additional languages (e.g. (Atserias et al., 1997; Vossen, 1998; Stamou et al., 2002)). Semantic resources can take many forms, but one of the most basic types is a dictionary that associates a word (or word sense) with one or more semantic categories (hypernyms). For example, *truck* might be identified as a VEHICLE, and *dog* might be identified as an ANIMAL. Automated methods for generating such dictionaries have been developed under the rubrics of lexical acquisition, hyponym learning, semantic class induction, and Web-based information extraction. These techniques can be used to rapidly create semantic lexicons for new domains and languages, and to automatically increase the coverage of existing resources.

Techniques for semantic lexicon induction can be subdivided into two groups: corpus-based methods and Web-based methods. Although the Web can be viewed as a (gigantic) corpus, these two approaches tend to have different goals. Corpus-based methods are typically designed to induce domain-specific semantic lexicons from a collection of domain-specific texts. In contrast, Web-based methods are typically designed to induce broad-coverage resources, similar to WordNet. Ideally, one would hope that broad-coverage resources would be sufficient for any domain, but this is often not the case. Many domains use specialized vocabularies and jargon that are not adequately represented in broad-coverage resources (e.g., medicine, genomics, etc.). Furthermore, even relatively general text genres, such as news, contain subdomains that require extensive knowledge of specific semantic categories. For example, our work uses a corpus of news articles about terrorism that includes many arcane weapon terms (e.g., *M-79*, *AR-15*, *an-fo*, and *gelignite*). Similarly, our disease-related documents mention obscure diseases (e.g., *psittacosis*) and contain many informal terms, abbreviations, and spelling variants that do not even occur in most medical dictionaries. For example, *yf* refers to yellow fever, *tularaemia* is an alternative spelling for *tularemia*, and *nv-cjd* is frequently used

Proceedings of the NAACL HLT Workshop on Unsupervised and Minimally Supervised Learning of Lexical Semantics, pages 18–26,
Boulder, Colorado, June 2009.

to refer to *new variant Creutzfeldt Jacob Disease*.

The Web is such a vast repository of knowledge that specialized terminology for nearly any domain probably exists in some niche or cranny, but finding the appropriate corner of the Web to tap into is a challenge. You have to know where to look to find specialized knowledge. In contrast, corpus-based methods can learn specialized terminology directly from a domain-specific corpus, but accuracy can be a problem because most corpora are relatively small.

In this paper, we seek to exploit the best of both worlds by combining a weakly supervised corpus-based method for semantic lexicon induction with statistics obtained from the Web. First, we use a bootstrapping algorithm, Basilisk (Thelen and Riloff, 2002), to automatically induce a semantic lexicon from a domain-specific corpus. This produces a set of words that are hypothesized to belong to the targeted semantic category. Second, we use the Web as a source of corroborating evidence to confirm, or disconfirm, whether each term truly belongs to the semantic category. For each candidate word, we search the Web for pages that contain both the word and a semantically related term. We expect that true semantic category members will co-occur with semantically similar words more often than non-members.

This paper is organized as follows. Section 2 discusses prior work on weakly supervised methods for semantic lexicon induction. Section 3 overviews our approach: we briefly describe the weakly supervised bootstrapping algorithm that we use for corpus-based semantic lexicon induction, and then present our procedure for gathering corroborating evidence from the Web. Section 4 presents experimental results on seven semantic categories representing two domains: Latin American terrorism and disease-related documents. Section 5 summarizes our results and discusses future work.

2 Related Work

Our research focuses on semantic lexicon induction, where the goal is to create a list of words that belong to a desired semantic class. A substantial amount of previous work has been done on weakly supervised and unsupervised creation of semantic lexicons. Weakly supervised corpus-based methods have utilized noun co-occurrence statistics (Riloff and Shepherd, 1997; Roark and Charniak, 1998), syntactic information (Widdows and Dorow, 2002; Phillips and Riloff, 2002; Pantel and Ravichandran, 2004; Tanev and Magnini, 2006), and lexico-syntactic contextual patterns (e.g., *"resides in <location>"* or *"moved to <location>"*) (Riloff and Jones, 1999; Thelen and Riloff, 2002). Due to the need for POS tagging and/or parsing, these types of methods have been evaluated only on fixed corpora[1], although (Pantel et al., 2004) demonstrated how to scale up their algorithms for the Web. The goal of our work is to improve upon corpus-based bootstrapping algorithms by using co-occurrence statistics obtained from the Web to re-rank and filter the hypothesized category members.

Techniques for semantic class learning have also been developed specifically for the Web. Several Web-based semantic class learners build upon Hearst's early work (Hearst, 1992) with hyponym patterns. Hearst exploited patterns that explicitly identify a hyponym relation between a semantic class and a word (e.g., *"such authors as <X>"*) to automatically acquire new hyponyms. (Paşca, 2004) applied hyponym patterns to the Web and learned semantic class instances and groups by acquiring contexts around the patterns. Later, (Pasca, 2007) created context vectors for a group of seed instances by searching Web query logs, and used them to learn similar instances. The KnowItAll system (Etzioni et al., 2005) also uses hyponym patterns to extract class instances from the Web and evaluates them further by computing mutual information scores based on Web queries. (Kozareva et al., 2008) proposed the use of a doubly-anchored hyponym pattern and a graph to represent the links between hyponym occurrences in these patterns.

Our work builds upon Turney's work on semantic orientation (Turney, 2002) and synonym learning (Turney, 2001), in which he used a PMI-IR algorithm to measure the similarity of words and phrases based on Web queries. We use a similar PMI (point-wise mutual information) metric for the purposes of semantic class verification.

There has also been work on fully unsupervised

[1]Meta-bootstrapping (Riloff and Jones, 1999) was evaluated on Web pages, but used a precompiled corpus of downloaded Web pages.

semantic clustering (e.g., (Lin, 1998; Lin and Pantel, 2002; Davidov and Rappoport, 2006; Davidov et al., 2007)), however clustering methods may or may not produce the types and granularities of semantic classes desired by a user. Another related line of work is automated ontology construction, which aims to create lexical hierarchies based on semantic classes (e.g., (Caraballo, 1999; Cimiano and Volker, 2005; Mann, 2002)).

3 Semantic Lexicon Induction with Web-based Corroboration

Our approach combines a weakly supervised learning algorithm for corpus-based semantic lexicon induction with a follow-on procedure that gathers corroborating statistical evidence from the Web. In this section, we describe both of these components. First, we give a brief overview of the Basilisk bootstrapping algorithm that we use for corpus-based semantic lexicon induction. Second, we present our new strategies for acquiring and utilizing corroborating statistical evidence from the Web.

3.1 Corpus-based Semantic Lexicon Induction via Bootstrapping

For corpus-based semantic lexicon induction, we use a weakly supervised bootstrapping algorithm called Basilisk (Thelen and Riloff, 2002). As input, Basilisk requires a small set of *seed words* for each semantic category, and a collection of (unannotated) texts. Basilisk iteratively generates new words that are hypothesized to belong to the same semantic class as the seeds. Here we give an overview of Basilisk's algorithm and refer the reader to (Thelen and Riloff, 2002) for more details.

The key idea behind Basilisk is to use pattern contexts around a word to identify its semantic class. Basilisk's bootstrapping process has two main steps: Pattern Pool Creation and Candidate Word Selection. First, Basilisk applies the AutoSlog pattern generator (Riloff, 1996) to create a set of lexicosyntactic patterns that, collectively, can extract every noun phrase in the corpus. Basilisk then ranks the patterns according to how often they extract the seed words, under the assumption that patterns which extract known category members are likely to extract other category members as well. The highest-ranked patterns are placed in a *pattern pool*.

Second, Basilisk gathers every noun phrase that is extracted by at least one pattern in the pattern pool, and designates each head noun as a *candidate* for the semantic category. The candidates are then scored and ranked. For each candidate, Basilisk collects all of the patterns that extracted that word, computes the logarithm of the number of seeds extracted by each of those patterns, and finally computes the average of these log values as the score for the candidate. Intuitively, a candidate word receives a high score if it was extracted by patterns that, on average, also extract many known category members.

The N highest ranked candidates are automatically added to the list of *seed words*, taking a leap of faith that they are true members of the semantic category. The bootstrapping process then repeats, using the larger set of seed words as known category members in the next iteration.

Basilisk learns many good category members, but its accuracy varies a lot across semantic categories (Thelen and Riloff, 2002). One problem with Basilisk, and bootstrapping algorithms in general, is that accuracy tends to deteriorate as bootstrapping progresses. Basilisk generates candidates by identifying the contexts in which they occur and words unrelated to the desired category can sometimes also occur in those contexts. Some patterns consistently extract members of several semantic classes; for example, *"attack on <NP>"* will extract both people (*"attack on the president"*) and buildings (*"attack on the U.S. embassy"*). Idiomatic expressions and parsing errors can also lead to undesirable words being learned. Incorrect words tend to accumulate as bootstrapping progresses, which can lead to gradually deteriorating performance.

(Thelen and Riloff, 2002) tried to address this problem by learning multiple semantic categories simultaneously. This helps to keep the bootstrapping focused by flagging words that are potentially problematic because they are strongly associated with a competing category. This improved Basilisk's accuracy, but by a relatively small amount, and this approach depends on the often unrealistic assumption that a word cannot belong to more than one semantic category. In our work, we use the single-category version of Basilisk that learns each semantic category independently so that we do not need to make this assumption.

3.2 Web-based Semantic Class Corroboration

The novel aspect of our work is that we introduce a new mechanism to independently verify each candidate word's category membership using the Web as an external knowledge source. We gather statistics from the Web to provide evidence for (or against) the semantic class of a word in a manner completely independent of Basilisk's criteria. Our approach is based on the *distributional hypothesis* (Harris, 1954), which says that words that occur in the same contexts tend to have similar meanings. We seek to corroborate a word's semantic class through statistics that measure how often the word co-occurs with semantically related words.

For each candidate word produced by Basilisk, we construct a Web query that pairs the word with a semantically related word. Our goal is not just to find Web pages that contain both terms, but to find Web pages that contain both terms in close proximity to one another. We consider two terms to be collocated if they occur within ten words of each other on the same Web page, which corresponds to the functionality of the NEAR operator used by the AltaVista search engine[2]. Turney (Turney, 2001; Turney, 2002) reported that the NEAR operator outperformed simple page co-occurrence for his purposes; our early experiments informally showed the same for this work.

We want our technique to remain weakly supervised, so we do not want to require additional human input or effort beyond what is already required for Basilisk. With this in mind, we investigated two types of collocation relations as possible indicators of semantic class membership:

Hypernym Collocation: We compute co-occurrence statistics between the candidate word and the name of the targeted semantic class (i.e., the word's hypothesized hypernym). For example, given the candidate word *jeep* and the semantic category VEHICLE, we would issue the Web query "*jeep* NEAR *vehicle*". Our intuition is that such queries would identify definition-type Web hits. For example, the query "*cow* NEAR *animal*" might retrieve snippets such as *"A cow is an animal found on dairy farms"* or *"An animal such as a cow has..."*.

Seed Collocation: We compute co-occurrence statistics between the candidate word and each seed word that was given to Basilisk as input. For example, given the candidate word *jeep* and the seed word *truck*, we would issue the Web query "*jeep* NEAR *truck*". Here the intuition is that members of the same semantic category tend to occur near one another - in lists, for example.

As a statistical measure of co-occurrence, we compute a variation of Pointwise Mutual Information (PMI), which is defined as:

$$PMI(x, y) = log(\frac{p(x,y)}{p(x)*p(y)})$$

where $p(x, y)$ is the probability that x and y are collocated (near each other) on a Web page, $p(x)$ is the probability that x occurs on a Web page, and $p(y)$ is the probability that y occurs on a Web page.

$p(x)$ is calculated as $\frac{count(x)}{N}$, where $count(x)$ is the number of hits returned by AltaVista, searching for x by itself, and N is the total number of documents on the World Wide Web at the time the query is made. Similarly, $p(x, y)$ is $\frac{count(x\ NEAR\ y)}{N}$. Given this, the PMI equation can be rewritten as:

$$log(N) + log(\frac{count(x\ NEAR\ y)}{count(x)*count(y)})$$

N is not known, but it is the same for every query (assuming the queries were made at roughly the same time). We will use these scores solely to compare the relative goodness of candidates, so we can omit N from the equation because it will not change the relative ordering of the scores. Thus, our PMI score[3] for a candidate word and related term (hypernym or seed) is:

$$log(\frac{count(x\ NEAR\ y)}{count(x)*count(y)})$$

Finally, we created three different scoring functions that use PMI values in different ways to capture different types of co-occurrence information:

Hypernym Score: PMI based on collocation between the hypernym term and candidate word.

[2]http://www.altavista.com

[3]In the rare cases when a term had a zero hit count, we assigned -99999 as the PMI score, which effectively ranks it at the bottom.

Average of Seeds Score: The mean of the PMI scores computed for the candidate and each seed word:

$$\frac{1}{|seeds|}\sum_{i=1}^{|seeds|} PMI(candidate, seed_i)$$

Max of Seeds Score: The maximum (highest) of the PMI scores computed for the candidate and each seed word.

The rationale for the Average of Seeds Score is that the seeds are all members of the semantic category, so we might expect other members to occur near many of them. Averaging over all of the seeds can diffuse unusually high or low collocation counts that might result from an anomalous seed. The rationale for the Max of Seeds Score is that a word may naturally co-occur with some category members more often than others. For example, one would expect *dog* to co-occur with *cat* much more frequently than with *frog*. A high Max of Seeds Score indicates that there is at least one seed word that frequently co-occurs with the candidate.

Since Web queries are relatively expensive, it is worth taking stock of how many queries are necessary. Let N be the number of candidate words produced by Basilisk, and S be the number of seed words given to Basilisk as input. To compute the Hypernym Score for a candidate, we need 3 queries: $count(hypernym)$, $count(candidate)$, and $count(hypernym\ NEAR\ candidate)$. The first query is the same for all candidates, so for N candidate words we need $2N + 1$ queries in total. To compute the Average or Max of Seeds Score for a candidate, we need S queries for $count(seed_i)$, S queries for $count(seed_i\ NEAR\ candidate)$, and 1 query for $count(candidate)$. So for N candidate words we need $N * (2S + 1)$ queries. S is typically small for weakly supervised algorithms (S=10 in our experiments), which means that this Web-based corroboration process requires $O(N)$ queries to process a semantic lexicon of size N.

4 Evaluation

4.1 Data Sets

We ran experiments on two corpora: 1700 MUC-4 terrorism articles (MUC-4 Proceedings, 1992) and a combination of 6000 disease-related documents, consisting of 2000 ProMed disease outbreak reports (ProMed-mail, 2006) and 4000 disease-related PubMed abstracts (PubMed, 2009). For the terrorism domain, we created lexicons for four semantic categories: BUILDING, HUMAN, LOCATION, and WEAPON. For the disease domain, we created lexicons for three semantic categories: ANIMAL[4], DISEASE, and SYMPTOM. For each category, we gave Basilisk 10 seed words as input. The seeds were chosen by applying a shallow parser to each corpus, extracting the head nouns of all the NPs, and sorting the nouns by frequency. A human then walked down the sorted list and identified the 10 most frequent nouns that belong to each semantic category[5]. This strategy ensures that the bootstrapping process is given seed words that occur in the corpus with high frequency. The seed words are shown in Table 1.

BUILDING:	embassy office headquarters church offices house home residence hospital airport
HUMAN:	people guerrillas members troops Cristiani rebels president terrorists soldiers leaders
LOCATION:	country El_Salvador Salvador United_States area Colombia city countries department Nicaragua
WEAPON:	weapons bomb bombs explosives arms missiles dynamite rifles materiel bullets
ANIMAL:	bird mosquito cow horse pig chicken sheep dog deer fish
DISEASE:	SARS BSE anthrax influenza WNV FMD encephalitis malaria pneumonia flu
SYMPTOM:	fever diarrhea vomiting rash paralysis weakness necrosis chills headaches hemorrhage

Table 1: Seed Words

To evaluate our results, we used the gold standard answer key that Thelen & Riloff created to evaluate Basilisk on the MUC4 corpus (Thelen and Riloff, 2002); they manually labeled every head noun in the corpus with its semantic class. For the ProMed / PubMed disease corpus, we created our own answer key. For all of the lexicon entries hypothesized by Basilisk, a human annotator (not any of the authors)

[4]ANIMAL was chosen because many of the ProMed disease outbreak stories concerned outbreaks among animal populations.

[5]The disease domain seed words were chosen from a larger set of ProMed documents, which included the 2000 used for lexicon induction.

	BUILDING				HUMAN				LOCATION				WEAPON			
N	Ba	Hy	Av	Mx	Ba	Hy	Av	Mx	Ba	Hy	Av	Mx	Ba	Hy	Av	Mx
25	.40	**.56**	.52	**.56**	.40	.72	.80	**.84**	.68	.88	.88	**1.0**	.56	.84	**1.0**	**1.0**
50	.44	**.56**	.46	.40	.56	.80	**.88**	.86	.80	.86	.84	**.98**	.52	.74	.76	**.90**
75	.44	**.45**	.41	.39	.65	.84	**.85**	**.85**	.80	.88	.80	**.99**	.52	.63	.65	**.79**
100	**.42**	.41	.38	.36	.69	.81	.80	**.87**	.81	.85	.78	**.95**	.55	.55	.56	**.63**
300	.22				.82				.75				.26			

	ANIMAL				DISEASE				SYMPTOM			
N	Ba	Hy	Av	Mx	Ba	Hy	Av	Mx	Ba	Hy	Av	Mx
25	.48	.88	**.92**	**.92**	.64	**.84**	.80	**.84**	.64	.84	**.92**	.80
50	.58	.82	**.84**	.80	.72	**.84**	.60	.82	.62	.76	**.90**	.74
75	.55	.68	.67	**.69**	.69	**.83**	.59	.81	.61	.68	**.79**	.71
100	.45	.55	.54	**.57**	.69	.78	.58	**.80**	.59	.71	**.77**	.64
300	.20				.62				.38			

Table 2: Ranking results for 7 semantic categories, showing accuracies for the top-ranked N words.
(Ba=Basilisk, Hy=Hypernym Re-ranking, Av=Average of Seeds Re-ranking, Mx=Max of Seeds Re-ranking

labeled each word as either correct or incorrect for the hypothesized semantic class. A word is considered to be correct if any sense of the word is semantically correct.

4.2 Ranking Results

We ran Basilisk for 60 iterations, learning 5 new words in each bootstrapping cycle, which produced a lexicon of 300 words for each semantic category. The columns labeled Ba in Table 2 show the accuracy results for Basilisk.[6] As we explained in Section 3.1, accuracy tends to decrease as bootstrapping progresses, so we computed accuracy scores for the top-ranked 100 words, in increments of 25, and also for the entire lexicon of 300 words.

Overall, we see that Basilisk learns many correct words for each semantic category, and the top-ranked terms are generally more accurate than the lower-ranked terms. For the top 100 words, accuracies are generally in the 50-70% range, except for LOCATION which achieves about 80% accuracy. For the HUMAN category, Basilisk obtained 82% accuracy over all 300 words, but the top-ranked words actually produced lower accuracy.

Basilisk's ranking is clearly not as good as it could be because there are correct terms co-mingled with incorrect terms throughout the ranked lists. This has two ramifications. First, if we want a human to manually review each lexicon before adding the words to an external resource, then the rankings may not be very helpful (i.e., the human will need to review all of the words), and (2) incorrect terms generated during the early stages of bootstrapping may be hindering the learning process because they introduce noise during bootstrapping. The HUMAN category seems to have recovered from early mistakes, but the lower accuracies for some other categories may be the result of this problem. The purpose of our Web-based corroboration process is to automatically re-evaluate the lexicons produced by Basilisk, using Web-based statistics to create more separation between the good entries and the bad ones.

Our first set of experiments uses the Web-based co-occurrence statistics to re-rank the lexicon entries. The Hy, Av, and Mx columns in Table 2 show the re-ranking results using each of the Hypernym, Average of Seeds, and Maximum of Seeds scoring functions. In all cases, Web-based re-ranking outperforms Basilisk's original rankings. Every semantic category except for BUILDING yielded accuracies of 80-100% among the top candidates. For each row, the highest accuracy for each semantic category is shown in boldface (as are any tied for highest).

Overall, the Max of Seeds Scores were best, performing better than or as well as the other scoring functions on 5 of the 7 categories. It was only out-

[6]These results are not comparable to the Basilisk results reported by (Thelen and Riloff, 2002) because our implementation only does single-category learning while the results in that paper are based on simultaneously learning multiple categories.

BUILDING	HUMAN	LOCATION	WEAPON	ANIMAL	DISEASE	SYMPTOM
consulate	guerrilla	San_Salvador	shotguns	bird-to-bird	meningo-encephalitis	nausea
pharmacies	extremists	Las_Hojas	carbines	cervids	bse).austria	diarrhoea
aiport	sympathizers	Tejutepeque	armaments	goats	inhalational	myalgias
zacamil	assassins	Ayutuxtepeque	revolvers	ewes	anthrax_disease	chlorosis
airports	patrols	Copinol	detonators	ruminants	otitis_media	myalgia
parishes	militiamen	Cuscatancingo	pistols	swine	airport_malaria	salivation
Masariegos	battalion	Jiboa	car_bombs	calf	taeniorhynchus	dysentery
chancery	Ellacuria	Chinameca	calibers	lambs	hyopneumonia	cramping
residences	rebel	Zacamil	M-16	wolsington	monkeypox	dizziness
police_station	policemen	Chalantenango	grenades	piglets	kala-azar	inappetance

Table 3: Top 10 words ranked by Max of Seeds Scores.

performed once by the Hypernym Scores (BUILDING) and once by the Average of Seeds Scores (SYMPTOM).

The strong performance of the Max of Seeds scores suggests that one seed is often an especially good collocation indicator for category membership – though it may not be the same seed word for all of the lexicon words. The relatively poor performance of the Average of Seeds scores may be attributable to the same principle; perhaps even if one seed is especially strong, averaging over the less-effective seeds' scores dilutes the results. Averaging is also susceptible to damage from words that receive the special-case score of -99999 when a hit count is zero (see Section 3.2).

Table 3 shows the 10 top-ranked candidates for each semantic category based on the Max of Seeds scores. The table illustrates that this scoring function does a good job of identifying semantically correct words, although of course there are some mistakes. Mistakes can happen due to parsing errors (e.g., *bird-to-bird* is an adjective and not a noun, as in *bird-to-bird transmission*), and some are due to issues associated with Web querying. For example, the nonsense term *"bse).austria"* was ranked highly because Altavista split this term into 2 separate words because of the punctuation, and *bse* by itself is indeed a disease term (*bovine spongiform encephalitis*).

4.3 Filtering Results

Table 2 revealed that the 300-word lexicons produced by Basilisk vary widely in the number of true category words that they contain. The least dense category is ANIMAL, with only 61 correct words, and the most dense is HUMAN with 247 correct words. Interestingly, the densest categories are not always the easiest to rank. For example, the HUMAN category is the densest category but Basilisk's ranking of the human terms was poor.

θ	*Category*	*Acc*	*Cor/Tot*
-22	WEAPON	**.88**	46/52
	LOCATION	**.98**	59/60
	HUMAN	.80	8/10
	BUILDING	**.83**	5/6
	ANIMAL	**.91**	30/33
	DISEASE	**.82**	64/78
	SYMPTOM	**.65**	64/99
-23	WEAPON	.79	59/75
	LOCATION	.96	82/85
	HUMAN	.85	23/27
	BUILDING	.71	12/17
	ANIMAL	.87	40/46
	DISEASE	.78	82/105
	SYMPTOM	.62	86/139
-24	WEAPON	.63	63/100
	LOCATION	.93	111/120
	HUMAN	**.87**	54/62
	BUILDING	.45	17/38
	ANIMAL	.75	47/63
	DISEASE	.74	94/127
	SYMPTOM	.60	100/166

Table 4: Filtering results using the Max of Seeds Scores.

The ultimate goal behind a better ranking mechanism is to completely automate the process of semantic lexicon induction. If we can produce high-quality rankings, then we can discard the lower ranked words and keep only the highest ranked words for our semantic dictionary. However, this presupposes that we know where to draw the line between the good and bad entries, and Table 2 shows that this boundary varies across categories. For HUMANS, the top 100 words are 87% accurate, and in fact we get 82% accuracy over all 300 words. But for ANIMALS we achieve 80% accuracy only for the top 50 words. It is paramount for semantic dictionaries to have high integrity, so accuracy must be high if we want to use the resulting lexicons without manual review.

As an alternative to ranking, another way that we could use the Web-based corroboration statistics is to automatically filter words that do not receive a high score. The key question is whether the values of the scores are consistent enough across categories to set a single threshold that will work well across the different categories.

Table 4 shows the results of using the Max of Seeds Scores as a filtering mechanism: given a threshold θ, all words that have a score $< \theta$ are discarded. For each threshold value θ and semantic category, we computed the accuracy (Acc) of the lexicon after all words with a score $< \theta$ have been removed. The Cor/Tot column shows the number of correct category members and the number of total words that passed the threshold.

We experimented with a variety of threshold values and found that θ=-22 performed best. Table 4 shows that this threshold produces a relatively high-precision filtering mechanism, with 6 of the 7 categories achieving lexicon accuracies $\geq$ 80%. As expected, the *Cor/Tot* column shows that the number of words varies widely across categories. Automatic filtering represents a trade-off: a relatively high-precision lexicon can be created, but some correct words will be lost. The threshold can be adjusted to increase the number of learned words, but with a corresponding drop in precision. Depending upon a user's needs, a high threshold may be desirable to identify only the most confident lexicon entries, or a lower threshold may be desirable to retain most of the correct entries while reliably removing some of the incorrect ones.

5 Conclusions

We have demonstrated that co-occurrence statistics gathered from the Web can dramatically improve the ranking of lexicon entries produced by a weakly-supervised corpus-based bootstrapping algorithm, without requiring any additional supervision. We found that computing Web-based co-occurrence statistics across a set of seed words and then using the highest score was the most successful approach. Co-occurrence with a hypernym term also performed well for some categories, and could be easily combined with the Max of Seeds approach by choosing the highest value among the seeds as well as the hypernym.

In future work, we would like to incorporate this Web-based re-ranking procedure into the bootstrapping algorithm itself to dynamically "clean up" the learned words before they are cycled back into the bootstrapping process. Basilisk could consult the Web-based statistics to select the best 5 words to generate before the next bootstrapping cycle begins. This integrated approach has the potential to substantially improve Basilisk's performance because it would improve the precision of the induced lexicon entries during the earliest stages of bootstrapping when the learning process is most fragile.

Acknowledgments

Many thanks to Julia James for annotating the gold standards for the disease domain. This research was supported in part by Department of Homeland Security Grant N0014-07-1-0152.

References

J. Atserias, S. Climent, X. Farreres, G. Rigau, and H. Rodriguez. 1997. Combining Multiple Methods for the Automatic Construction of Multilingual WordNets. In *Proceedings of the International Conference on Recent Advances in Natural Language Processing*.

S. Caraballo. 1999. Automatic Acquisition of a Hypernym-Labeled Noun Hierarchy from Text. In *Proc. of the 37th Annual Meeting of the Association for Computational Linguistics*, pages 120–126.

P. Cimiano and J. Volker. 2005. Towards large-scale, open-domain and ontology-based named entity classification. In *Proc. of Recent Advances in Natural Language Processing*, pages 166–172.

D. Davidov and A. Rappoport. 2006. Efficient unsupervised discovery of word categories using symmetric patterns and high frequency words. In *Proc. of the 21st International Conference on Computational Linguistics and the 44th annual meeting of the ACL.*

D. Davidov, A. Rappoport, and M. Koppel. 2007. Fully unsupervised discovery of concept-specific relationships by web mining. In *Proc. of the 45th Annual Meeting of the Association of Computational Linguistics*, pages 232–239, June.

O. Etzioni, M. Cafarella, D. Downey, A. Popescu, T. Shaked, S. Soderland, D. Weld, and A. Yates. 2005. Unsupervised named-entity extraction from the web: an experimental study. *Artificial Intelligence*, 165(1):91–134, June.

Z. Harris. 1954. Distributional Structure. In J. A. Fodor and J. J. Katz, editor, *The Structure of Language*, pages 33–49. Prentice-Hall.

M. Hearst. 1992. Automatic acquisition of hyponyms from large text corpora. In *Proc. of the 14th International Conference on Computational Linguistics (COLING-92)*.

Z. Kozareva, E. Riloff, and E. Hovy. 2008. Semantic Class Learning from the Web with Hyponym Pattern Linkage Graphs. In *Proceedings of the 46th Annual Meeting of the Association for Computational Linguistics: Human Language Technologies (ACL-08)*.

D. Lin and P. Pantel. 2002. Concept discovery from text. In *Proc. of the 19th International Conference on Computational linguistics*, pages 1–7.

D. Lin. 1998. Dependency-based Evaluation of MINIPAR. In *Workshop on the Evaluation of Parsing Systems, Granada, Spain*.

G. Mann. 2002. Fine-grained proper noun ontologies for question answering. In *Proc. of the 19th International Conference on Computational Linguistics*, pages 1–7.

G. Miller. 1990. Wordnet: An On-line Lexical Database. *International Journal of Lexicography*, 3(4).

MUC-4 Proceedings. 1992. *Proceedings of the Fourth Message Understanding Conference (MUC-4)*. Morgan Kaufmann.

M. Paşca. 2004. Acquisition of categorized named entities for web search. In *Proc. of the Thirteenth ACM International Conference on Information and Knowledge Management*, pages 137–145.

P. Pantel and D. Ravichandran. 2004. Automatically labeling semantic classes. In *Proc. of Conference of HLT / North American Chapter of the Association for Computational Linguistics*, pages 321–328.

P. Pantel, D. Ravichandran, and E. Hovy. 2004. Towards terascale knowledge acquisition. In *Proc. of the 20th international conference on Computational Linguistics*, page 771.

M. Pasca. 2007. weakly-supervised Discovery of Named Entities using Web Search Queries. In *CIKM*, pages 683–690.

W. Phillips and E. Riloff. 2002. Exploiting Strong Syntactic Heuristics and Co-Training to Learn Semantic Lexicons. In *Proceedings of the 2002 Conference on Empirical Methods in Natural Language Processing*, pages 125–132.

ProMed-mail. 2006. *http://www.promedmail.org/.*

PubMed. 2009. *http://www.ncbi.nlm.nih.gov/sites/entrez.*

E. Riloff and R. Jones. 1999. Learning Dictionaries for Information Extraction by Multi-Level Bootstrapping. In *Proceedings of the Sixteenth National Conference on Artificial Intelligence*.

E. Riloff and J. Shepherd. 1997. A Corpus-Based Approach for Building Semantic Lexicons. In *Proceedings of the Second Conference on Empirical Methods in Natural Language Processing*, pages 117–124.

E. Riloff. 1996. Automatically Generating Extraction Patterns from Untagged Text. In *Proceedings of the Thirteenth National Conference on Artificial Intelligence*, pages 1044–1049. The AAAI Press/MIT Press.

B. Roark and E. Charniak. 1998. Noun-phrase Co-occurrence Statistics for Semi-automatic Semantic Lexicon Construction. In *Proceedings of the 36th Annual Meeting of the Association for Computational Linguistics*, pages 1110–1116.

Sofia Stamou, Kemal Oflazer, Karel Pala, Dimitris Christoudoulakis, Dan Cristea, Dan Tufis, Svetla Koeva, George Totkov, Dominique Dutoit, and Maria Grigoriadou. 2002. Balkanet: A multilingual semantic network for the balkan languages. In *Proceedings of the 1st Global WordNet Association conference*.

H. Tanev and B. Magnini. 2006. Weakly supervised approaches for ontology population. In *Proc. of 11st Conference of the European Chapter of the Association for Computational Linguistics*.

M. Thelen and E. Riloff. 2002. A Bootstrapping Method for Learning Semantic Lexicons Using Extraction Pa ttern Contexts. In *Proceedings of the 2002 Conference on Empirical Methods in Natural Language Processing*, pages 214–221.

Peter D. Turney. 2001. Mining the Web for Synonyms: PMI-IR versus LSA on TOEFL. In *EMCL '01: Proceedings of the 12th European Conference on Machine Learning*, pages 491–502, London, UK. Springer-Verlag.

P. D. Turney. 2002. Thumbs up or thumbs down? semantic orientation applied to unsupervised classification of reviews. In *Proceedings of the 40th Annual Meeting of the Association for Computational Linguistics (ACL'02)*, pages 417–424.

Piek Vossen, editor. 1998. *EuroWordNet: A Multilingual Database with Lexical Semantic Networks*. Kluwer Academic Publishers, Norwell, MA, USA.

D. Widdows and B. Dorow. 2002. A graph model for unsupervised lexical acquisition. In *Proc. of the 19th International Conference on Computational Linguistics*, pages 1–7.

Cross-lingual Predicate Cluster Acquisition to Improve Bilingual Event Extraction by Inductive Learning

Heng Ji
Computer Science Department
Queens College and The Graduate Center
The City University of New York
hengji@cs.qc.cuny.edu

Abstract

In this paper we present two approaches to automatically extract cross-lingual predicate clusters, based on bilingual parallel corpora and cross-lingual information extraction. We demonstrate how these clusters can be used to improve the NIST Automatic Content Extraction (ACE) event extraction task[1]. We propose a new *inductive learning* framework to automatically augment background data for low-confidence events and then conduct global inference. Without using any additional data or accessing the baseline algorithms this approach obtained significant improvement over a state-of-the-art bilingual (English and Chinese) event extraction system.

1 Introduction

Event extraction, the 'classical' information extraction (IE) task, has progressed from Message Understanding Conference (MUC)-style single template extraction to the more comprehensive multi-lingual Automatic Content Extraction (ACE) extraction including more fine-grained types. This extension has made event extraction more widely applicable in many NLP tasks including cross-lingual document retrieval (Hakkani-Tur et al., 2007) and question answering (Schiffman et al., 2007). Various supervised learning approaches have been explored for ACE multi-lingual event extraction (e.g. Grishman et al., 2005; Ahn, 2006; Hardy et al., 2006; Tan et al., 2008; Chen and Ji, 2009). All of these previous literatures showed that one main bottleneck of event extraction lies in low recall. It's a challenging task to recognize the different forms in which an event may be expressed, given the limited amount of training data. The goal of this paper is to improve the performance of a bilingual (English and Chinese) state-of-the-art event extraction system without accessing its internal algorithms or annotating additional data.

As for a separate research theme, extensive techniques have been used to produce word clusters or paraphrases from large unlabeled corpora (Brown et al., 1990; Pereira et al., 1993; Lee and Pereira, 1999, Barzilay and McKeown, 2001; Lin and Pantel, 2001; Ibrahim et al., 2003; Pang et al., 2003). For example, (Bannard and Callison-Burch, 2005) and (Callison-Burch, 2008) described a method to extract paraphrases from largely available bilingual corpora. The resulting clusters contain words with similar semantic information and therefore can be useful to augment a small amount of annotated data. We will automatically extract cross-lingual predicate clusters using two different approaches based on bilingual parallel corpora and cross-lingual IE respectively; and then use the derived clusters to improve event extraction.

We propose a new learning method called *inductive learning* to exploit the derived predicate clusters. For each test document, a background document is constructed by gradually replacing the low-confidence events with the predicates in the same cluster. Then we conduct cross-document inference technique as described in (Ji and Grish-

[1] http://www.nist.gov/speech/tests/ace/

Proceedings of the NAACL HLT Workshop on Unsupervised and Minimally Supervised Learning of Lexical Semantics, pages 27–35,
Boulder, Colorado, June 2009.

man, 2008) to improve the performance of event extraction. This inductive learning approach matches the procedure of human knowledge acquisition and foreign language education: analyze information from specific examples and then discover a pattern or draw a conclusion; attempt synonyms to convey/learn the meaning of an intricate word.

The rest of this paper is structured as follows. Section 2 describes the terminology used in this paper. Section 3 presents the overall system architecture and the baseline system. Section 4 then describes in detail the approaches of extracting cross-lingual predicate clusters. Section 5 describes the motivations of using cross-lingual clusters to improve event extraction. Section 6 presents an overview of the inductive learning algorithm. Section 7 presents the experimental results. Section 8 compares our approach with related work and Section 9 then concludes the paper and sketches our future work.

2 Terminology

The event extraction task we are addressing is that of ACE evaluations. ACE defines the following terminology:

entity: an object or a set of objects in one of the semantic categories of interest
mention: a reference to an entity (typically, a noun phrase)
event trigger: the main word which most clearly expresses an event occurrence
event arguments: the mentions that are involved in an event (participants)
event mention: a phrase or sentence within which an event is described, including trigger and arguments

The 2005 ACE evaluation had 8 types of events, with 33 subtypes; for the purpose of this paper, we will treat these simply as 33 distinct event types. For example, for a sentence "*Barry Diller on Wednesday quit as chief of Vivendi Universal Entertainment*", the event extractor should detect all the following information: a "*Personnel_End-Position*" event mention, with "*quit*" as the trigger word, "*chief*" as an argument with a *role* of "position", "*Barry Diller*" as the person who quit the position, "*Vivendi Universal Entertainment*" as the organization, and the time during which the event happened is "*Wednesday*".

3 Approach Overview

3.1 System Pipeline

Figure 1 depicts the general procedure of our approach. The set of test event mentions is improved by exploiting cross-lingual predicate clusters.

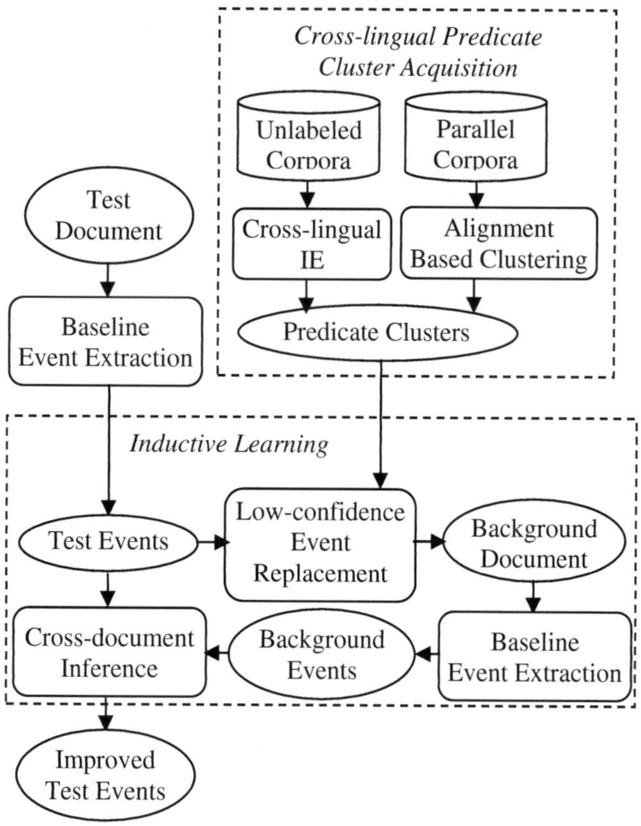

Figure 1. System Overview

The following section 3.2 will give more details about the baseline bilingual event tagger. Then we will present the predicate cluster acquisition algorithm in section 4 and the method of exploiting clusters for event extraction in section 6.

3.2 A Baseline Bilingual Event Extraction System

We use a state-of-the-art bi-lingual event extraction system (Grishman et al., 2005; Chen and Ji, 2009) as our baseline. The system combines pattern matching with a set of Maximum Entropy classifiers: to distinguish events from non-events;

to classify events by type and subtype; to distinguish arguments from non-arguments; to classify arguments by argument role; and given a trigger, an event type, and a set of arguments, to determine whether there is a reportable event mention. In addition, the Chinese system incorporates some language-specific features to address the problem of word segmentation (Chen and Ji, 2009).

4 Cross-lingual Predicate Cluster Acquisition

We start from two different approaches to extract cross-lingual predicate clusters, based on parallel corpora and cross-lingual IE techniques respectively.

4.1 Acquisition from Bilingual Parallel Corpora

In the first approach, we take use of the 852 Chinese event trigger words in ACE05 training corpora as our 'anchor set'. For each Chinese trigger, we search its automatically aligned English words from a Chinese-English parallel corpus including 50,000 sentence pairs (part of Global Autonomous Language Exploitation Y3 Machine Translation training corpora) to construct an English predicate cluster. The word alignment was obtained by running Giza++ (Och and Ney, 2003). In each cluster we record the frequency of each unique English word. Then we conduct the same procedure in the other direction to construct Chinese predicate clusters anchored by English triggers.

State-of-the-art Chinese-English word alignment error rate is about 40% (Deng and Byrne, 2005). Therefore the resulting cross-lingual clusters include a lot of word alignment errors. In order to address this problem, we filter the clusters by only keeping those predicates including the original predicate forms in ACE training data or English/Chinese Propbank (Palmer et al., 2005; Xue and Palmer, 2009).

4.2 Acquisition from Cross-lingual IE

Based on the intuition that Machine Translation (MT) may translate a Chinese trigger word into different English words in different contexts, we employ the second approach using cross-lingual IE techniques (Hakkani-Tur et al., 2007) on TDT5 Chinese corpus to generate more clusters. We apply the following two cross-lingual IE pipelines:

Chinese IE_MT: Apply Chinese IE on the Chinese texts to get a set of Chinese triggers *ch-trigger-set1*, and then use word alignments to translate (project) *ch-trigger-set1* into a set of English triggers *en-trigger-set1*;

MT_English IE: Translate Chinese texts into English, and then apply English IE on the translated texts to get a set of English triggers *en-trigger-set2*.

For any Chinese trigger *ch-trigger* in *ch-trigger-set1*, if its corresponding translation *en-trigger* in *en-trigger-set1* is the same as that in *en-trigger-set2*, then we add *en-trigger* into the cluster anchored by *ch-trigger*.

We apply the English and Chinese IE systems as described in (Grishman et al., 2005; Chen and Ji, 2009). Both cross-lingual IE pipelines need machine translation to translate Chinese documents (for English IE) or project the extraction results from Chinese IE into English. We use the RWTH Aachen Chinese-to-English statistical phrase-based machine translation system (Zens and Ney, 2004) for these purposes.

4.3 Derived Cross-lingual Predicate Clusters

Applying the above two approaches we obtained 438 English predicate clusters and 543 Chinese predicate clusters.

For example, for a trigger "伤(injure)", we can get the following two predicate clusters with their frequency in the parallel corpora:

伤→{injured:99 injuries:96 injury:76 wounded:38 wounding:28 injuring:14 wounds:7 killed:4 died:2 mutilated:1 casualties:1 chop:1 killing:1 shot:1}.

injured →{受伤:1624 重伤:102 伤:99 轻伤:29 伤势:23 炸:12 打伤:10 爆炸:6 伤害:3 死亡:2 冲突:1 亡:1 烫伤:1 损失:1 出席:1 登陆:1 致残:1 自残:1 }

We can see that the predicates in the same cluster are not restrictedly synonyms, but they were generated as alternative translations for the same word and therefore represent similar meanings. More importantly, these triggers vary from very common ones such as 'injured' to rare words such as 'mutilate'. This indicates how these clusters can aid extracting low-confidence events: when deciding whether a word 'mutilate' indicates a "Life-

Injure" event in a certain context, we can replace it with other predicates in the same cluster and may provide us more reliable overall evidence.

Figure 2 presents the distribution of clusters which include more than one predicate.

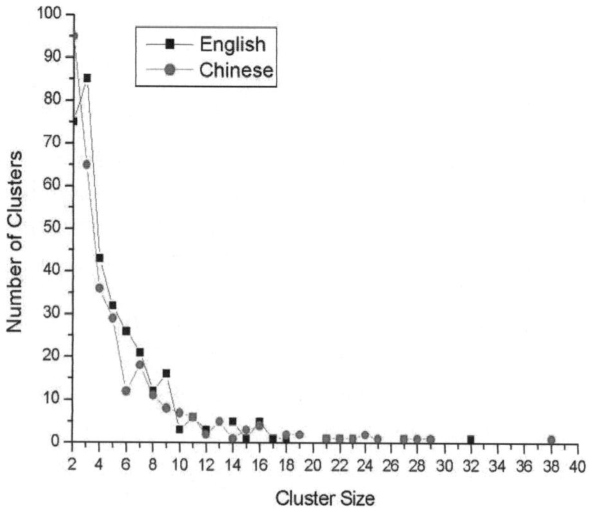

Figure 2. Cluster Size Distribution

We can see that most clusters include 2-9 predicates in both English and Chinese. However on average English clusters include more predicates. In addition, there are many more singletons in Chinese (232) than in English (101). This indicates that Chinese event triggers are more ambiguous.

5 Motivation of Using Cross-lingual Clusters for Event Extraction

After extracting cross-lingual predicate clusters, we can combine the evidence from all the predicates in each cluster to adjust the probabilities of event labeling. In the following we present some examples in both languages to demonstrate this motivation.

5.1 Improve Rare Trigger Labeling

Due to the limited training data, many trigger words only appear a few times as a particular type of event. This data sparse problem directly leads to the low recall of trigger labeling. But exploiting the evidence from other predicates in the same cluster may boost the confidence score of the candidate event. We present two examples as follows.

(1) English Example 1

For example, "*blown up*" doesn't appear in the training data as a "Conflict-Attack" event, and so it cannot be identified in the following test sentence. However, if we replace it with other predicates in the same cluster, the system can easily identify 'Conflict-Attack' events in the new sentences with high confidence values:

(a) Test Sentence:
Identified as "Conflict-Attack" Event with Confidence=0:

He told AFP that Israeli intelligence had been dealing with at least 40 tip-offs of impending attacks when the Haifa bus was ***blown up****.*

(b) Cross-lingual Cluster
炸毁 → *{* ***blown up****:4 bombing:3 blew:2 destroying:1 destroyed:1 }*

(c) Replaced Sentences
Identified as "Conflict-Attack" Event with Confidence=0.799:

He told AFP that Israeli intelligence had been dealing with at least 40 tip-offs of impending attacks when the Haifa bus was ***destroyed****.*

...

(2) Chinese Example 1

Chinese predicate clusters anchored by English words can also provide external evidence for event identification. For example, the trigger word "假释 (release/parole)" appears rarely in the Chinese training data but in most cases it can be replaced by a more frequent trigger "释放(release)" to represent the same meaning. Therefore by combining the evidence from "释放" we can enhance the confidence value of identifying "假释" as a "Justice-Release_Parole" event. For example,

(a) Test Sentence:
Identified as "Justice-Release_Parole" Event with Confidence=0:

*这名嫌犯因为侵害案件****假释****出狱却又犯下了重罪。(This suspect was released because of the violation case but committed a felony again.)*

(b) Cross-lingual Cluster
*releasing →{ **假释**:4 释放:1 }*

(c) Replaced Sentences
Identified as "Justice-Release_Parole" Event with Confidence=0.964:

*这名嫌犯因为侵害案件**释放**出狱却又犯下了重罪.*
...

5.2 Improve Frequent Trigger Labeling

On the other hand, some common words are highly ambiguous in particular contexts. But the other less-ambiguous predicates in the clusters can help classify event types more accurately.

(1) English Example 2

For example, in the following sentence the "*Personnel-End_Position*" event is missing because "*step*" doesn't indicate any ACE events in the training data. However, after replacing "step" with other prediates such as "quit", the system can identify the event more easily:

(a) Test Sentence:
Identified as "Personnel-End_Position" Event with Confidence=0:

*Barry Diller on Wednesday **step** from chief of Vivendi Universal Entertainment, the entertainment unit of French giant Vivendi Universal.*

(b) Cross-lingual Cluster
*下台 →{ resign:6 **step**:5 quit:3}*

(c) Replaced Sentences
Classified as "Personnel-End_Position" Event with Confidence=0.564:

*Barry Diller on Wednesday **quit** from chief of Vivendi Universal Entertainment, the entertainment unit of French giant Vivendi Universal.*
...

(2) Chinese Example 2

Some single-character Chinese predicates can represent many different event types in different contexts. For example, the word "打" appears in 27 different predicate clusters, representing the meaning of hit/call/strike/form/take/draw etc. Therefore we can take use of other less ambiguous predicates in these clusters to adjust the likelihood of event classification.

For example, in the following test sentence, the word "打" indicates two different event types. If we replace these words with other predicates, we can classify them into different event types more accurately based on the evidence from replaced predicates and contexts.

(a) Test Sentence:
Event Classification for trigger word "打":

*就在几天前船长紧急**打 ("call", Phone-Write event with confidence 0)** 电报求救，表示轮机长蔡明志已经在 10 天前被大陆渔工**打("attacked/killed", Conflict-Attack event with confidence 0.528)**死，自己也被殴**打("attacked", Conflict-Attack event with confidence 0.946)**，连人带船胁持到大陆。(Several days ago the Captain **called** urgent telegraphs to ask for help, expressing that the boat pilot Cai Mingzhi was already **killed** by mainland fishermen and he himself was **assaulted** and duressed to the mainland.)*

(b) Cross-lingual Cluster

*call→{ 打电话:6 电话:6 **打:1** 拨打:1 }*

*attack→{ 袭击:564 进攻:110 攻击:114 打击:24 反击:15 爆炸:15 突袭:15 击:8 偷:6 围攻:6 身亡:5 行凶:4 战争:3 死亡:3 丧生:2 谋杀:2 死:2 轰炸:2 侵略:2 入侵:2 设立:1 出兵:1 推翻:1 打死:1 劫持:1 **打:1** 遇害:1 咬:1 }*

(c) Replaced Sentences
Event Classification for trigger word "打" with higher confidence:

*就在几天前船长紧急**拨打 ("call", Phone-Write event with confidence 0.938)** 电报求救，表示轮机长蔡明志已经在 10 天前被大陆渔工杀 **("attacked/killed", Conflict-Attack event with confidence 0.583)**死，自己也被**袭击("attacked", Conflict-Attack event with confidence 0.987)**，连人带船胁持到大陆。*
...

Based on the above motivations we propose to incorporate cross-lingual predicate clusters to refine event identification and classification. In order to exploit these clusters effectively, we shall generate additional background data and conduct global confidence. The sections below will present the detailed algorithms.

6 Inductive Learning

We design a framework of inductive learning to incorporate the derived predicate clusters. The general idea of inductive learning is to analyze information from all kinds of specific examples until we can draw a conclusion. Since the main goal of our approach is to improve the recall of event extraction, we shall focus on those events generated by the baseline tagger with low confidence. For those events we automatically generate background documents using the predicate clusters (details in section 6.1) and then conduct global inference between each test document and its background documents (section 6.2).

6.1 Background Document Generation

For each event mention in a test document, the baseline event tagger produces the following local confidence value:

- *LConf(trigger, etype)*: The probability of a string *trigger* indicating an event mention with type *etype* in a context sentence *S*;

If *LConf(trigger, etype)* is lower than a threshold, and it belongs to a predicate cluster *C*, we create an additional background document *BD* by:

- For each $predicate_i \in C$, we replace *trigger* with $predicate_i$ in *S* to generate new sentence *S'*, and add *S'* into *BD*.

6.2 Global Inference

For each background document *BD*, we apply the baseline event extraction and get a set of background events. We then apply the cross-document inference techniques as described in (Ji and Grishman, 2008) to improve trigger and argument labeling performance by favoring interpretation consistency across the test events and background events.

This approach is based on the premise that many events will be reported multiple times from different sources in different forms. This naturally occurs in the test document and the background document because they include triggers from the same predicate cluster.

By aggregating events across each pair of test document *TD* and background document *BD*, we conduct the following statistical global inference:

- to remove triggers and arguments with low confidence in *TD* and *BD*;
- to adjust trigger and argument identification and classification to achieve consistency across *TD* and *BD*.

In this way we can propagate highly consistent and frequent triggers and arguments with high global confidence to override other, lower confidence, extraction results.

7 Experimental Results

7.1 Data and Scoring Metric

We used ACE2005 English and Chinese training corpora to evaluate our approach. Table 1 shows the number of documents used for training, development and blind testing.

Language	Training Set	Development Set	Test Set
English	525	33	66
Chinese	500	10	40

Table 1. Number of Documents

We define the following standards to determine the *correctness* of an event mention:

- *A trigger is correctly identified* if its position in the document matches a reference trigger.
- *A trigger is correctly identified and classified* if its event type and position in the document match a reference trigger.
- *An argument is correctly identified* if its event type and position in the document match any of the reference argument mentions.
- *An argument is correctly identified and classified* if its event type, position in the document, and role match any of the reference argument mentions.

Language/System (Performance)		Trigger Identification +Classification			Argument Identification			Argument Classification Accuracy	Argument Identification +Classification		
		P	R	F	P	R	F		P	R	F
English	Baseline	67.8	53.5	59.8	49.3	31.4	38.3	88.2	43.5	27.7	33.9
	After Using Cross-lingual Predicate Clusters	**69.2**	**59.4**	**63.9**	**51.7**	**32.7**	**40.1**	**89.6**	**46.3**	**29.3**	**35.9**
Chinese	Baseline	58.1	47.2	52.1	46.2	33.7	39.0	95.0	43.9	32.0	37.0
	After Using Cross-lingual Predicate Clusters	**60.2**	**52.6**	**56.1**	**46.8**	**36.7**	**41.1**	**95.6**	**44.7**	**35.1**	**39.3**

Table 2. Overall Performance on Blind Test Set (%)

7.2 Confidence Metric Thresholding

Before blind testing we select the thresholds for the trigger confidence *LConf(trigger, etype)* as defined in section 6.1 by optimizing the F-measure score of on the development set. Figure 3 shows the effect on precision and recall of varying the threshold for inductive learning using cross-lingual predicate clusters.

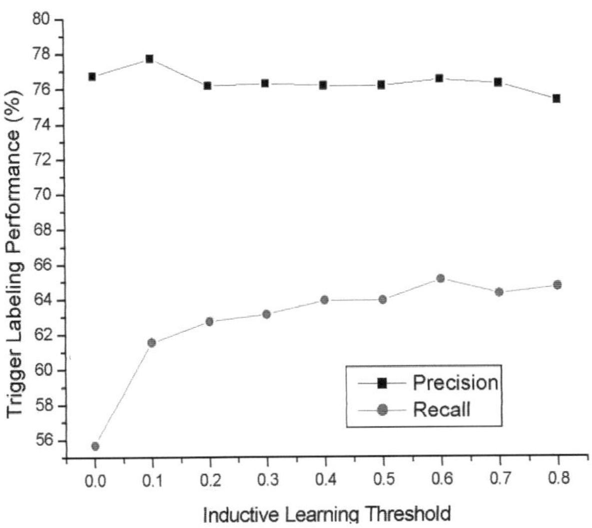

Figure 3. Trigger Labeling Performance with Inductive Learning Confidence Thresholding on English Development Set

We can see that the best performance on the development set can be obtained by selecting threshold 0.6, achieving 9.4% better recall with a little loss in precision (0.26%) compared to the baseline (with threshold=0) . Then we apply this threshold value directly for blind test. This optimizing procedure is repeated for Chinese as well.

7.3 Overall Performance

Table 2 shows the overall Precision (P), Recall (R) and F-Measure (F) scores for the blind test set.

For both English and Chinese, the inductive learning approach using cross-lingual predicate clusters provided significant improvement over the baseline event extraction system (about 4% absolute improvement on trigger labeling and 2%-2.3% on argument labeling). The most significant gain was provided for the recall of trigger labeling – 5.9% absolute improvement for English and 5.4% absolute improvement for Chinese.

Surprisingly this approach didn't cause any loss in precision. In fact small gains were obtained on precision for both languages. This indicates that cross-lingual predicate clusters are effective at adjusting the confidence values so that the events were not over-generated. The refined event trigger labeling also directly yields better performance in argument labeling.

We conducted the Wilcoxon Matched-Pairs Signed-Ranks Test on a document basis. The results show that for both languages the improvement using cross-lingual predicate clusters is significant at a 99.7% confidence level for trigger labeling and a 96.4% confidence level for argument labeling.

7.4 Discussion

For comparison we attempted a self-training approach: adding high-confidence events in the test set back as additional training data and re-train the event tagger. This produced 1.7% worse F-measure score for the English development set. It further proves that using the test set itself is not enough, we need to explore new predicates to serve as background evidence.

In addition we also applied a bootstrapping approach using relevant unlabeled data and obtained limited improvement – about 1.6% F-measure gain for English. As Ji and Grishman (2006) pointed out, both self-training and bootstrapping methods require good data selection scheme. But not for any test set we can easily find relevant unlabeled data. Therefore the approach presented in this paper is less expensive – we can automatically generate background data while introducing new evidence.

An alternative way of incorporating the cross-lingual predicate clusters would follow (Miller et al., 2004), namely encoding the cluster membership as an additional feature in the supervised-learning procedure of the baseline event tagger. However in the situation where we cannot directly change the algorithms of the baseline system, our approach of inductive learning is more flexible.

8 Related Work

Our approach of extracting predicate clusters is related to some prior work on paraphrase or word cluster discovery, either from mono-lingual parallel corpora (e.g. Barzilay and McKeown, 2001; Lin and Pantel, 2001; Ibrahim et al., 2003; Pang et al., 2003) or cross-lingual parallel corpora (e.g. Bannard and Callison-Burch, 2005; Callison-Burch, 2008). Shinyama and Sekine (2003) presented an approach of extracting paraphrases using names, dates and numbers as anchors. Hasegawa et al. (2004) described a paraphrase discovery approach based on clustering concurrent name pairs.

Several recent studies have stressed the benefits of using paraphrases or word clusters to improve IE components. For example, (Miller et al., 2004) proved that word clusters can significantly improve English name tagging. The idea of using predicates in the same cluster for candidate trigger replacement is similar to Ge et al.(1998) who used local context replacement for pronoun resolution. To the best of our knowledge, our work presented the first experiment of using cross-lingual predicate paraphrases for the ACE event extraction task.

9 Conclusion and Future Work

In this paper we described two approaches to extract cross-lingual predicate clusters, and designed a new inductive learning framework to effectively incorporate these clusters for event extraction. Without using any additional data or changing the baseline algorithms, we demonstrated that this method can significantly enhance the performance of a state-of-the-art bilingual event tagger.

We have noticed that the current filtering scheme based on Propbank may be too restricted to keep enough informative predicates. In the future we will attempt incorporating POS tagging results and frequency information.

In addition we will extend this framework to extract cross-lingual relation and name clusters to improve other IE tasks such as name tagging, relation extraction, event coreference and event translation. We are also interested in automatically discovering new event types (non-ACE event types) or more fine-grained subtypes/attributes for existing ACE event types from the derived predicate clusters.

Acknowledgments

This material is based upon work supported by the Defense Advanced Research Projects Agency under Contract No. HR0011-06-C-0023 via 27-001022, and the CUNY Research Enhancement Program and GRTI Program.

References

David Ahn. 2006. The stages of event extraction. *Proc. COLING/ACL 2006 Workshop on Annotating and Reasoning about Time and Events*. Sydney, Australia.

Colin Bannard and Chris Callison-Burch. 2005. Paraphrasing with Bilingual Parallel Corpora. *Proc. ACL 2005*.

Regina Barzilay and Kathleen McKeown. 2001. Extracting Paraphrases from a Parallel Corpus. *Proc. ACL 2001*.

Peter F. Brown, Vinvent J. Della pietra, Peter V. deSouza, Jenifer C. Lai, Robert L. Mercer. 1990. Class-based N-gram Models of Natural Language. *Computational Linguistics*.

Chris Callison-Burch. 2008. Syntactic Constraints on Paraphrases Extracted from Parallel Corpora. *Proc. EMNLP 2008*. Honolulu, USA.

Zheng Chen and Heng Ji. 2009. Language Specific Issue and Feature Exploration in Chinese Event Extraction. *Proc. HLT-NAACL 2009*. Boulder, Co.

Yonggang Deng and William Byrne. 2005. HMM Word and Phrase Alignment for Statistical Machine Translation. *Proc. HLT-EMNLP 2005*. Vancouver, Cananda.

Niyu Ge, John Hale and Eugene Charniak. 1998. A Statistical Approach to Anaphora Resolution. Proc. Sixth Workshop on Very Large Corpora

Ralph Grishman, David Westbrook and Adam Meyers. 2005. NYU's English ACE 2005 System Description. *Proc. ACE 2005 Evaluation Workshop*. Washington, US.

Dilek Hakkani-Tur, Heng Ji and Ralph Grishman. 2007. Using Information Extraction to Improve Cross-lingual Document Retrieval. *Proc. RANLP2007 workshop on Multi-source, Multilingual Information Extraction and Summarization*.

Hilda Hardy, Vika Kanchakouskaya and Tomek Strzalkowski. 2006. Automatic Event Classification Using Surface Text Features. *Proc. AAAI06 Workshop on Event Extraction and Synthesis*. Boston, Massachusetts. US.

Takaaki Hasegawa, Satoshi Sekine and Ralph Grishman. 2004. Discovering Relations among Named Entities from Large Corpora. *Proc. ACL 2004*. Barcelona, Spain.

Ali Ibrahim, Boris Katz and Jimmy Lin. 2003. Extracting Structural Paraphrases from Aligned Monolingual Corpora. *Proc. ACL 2003*.

Heng Ji and Ralph Grishman. 2006. Data Selection in Semi-supervised Learning for Name Tagging. *Proc. ACL 2006 Workshop on Information Extraction Beyond the Document*. Sydney, Australia.

Heng Ji and Ralph Grishman. 2008. Refining Event Extraction Through Cross-document Inference. *Proc. ACL 2008*. Ohio, USA

Lillian Lee and Fernando Pereira. 1999. Distributional Similarity Models: Clustering vs. Nearest Neighbors. *Proc. ACL1999*. pp. 33-40.

Dekang Lin and Patrick Pantel. 2001. DIRT-Discovery of Inference Rules from Text. *Proc. ACM SIGDD Conference on Knowledge Discovery and Data Mining*.

Scott Miller, Jethran Guinness and Alex Zamanian.2004. Name Tagging with Word Clusters and Discriminative Training. *Proc. HLT-NAACL2004*. pp. 337-342. Boston, USA.

Franz Josef Och and Hermann Ney. 2003. "A Systematic Comparison of Various Statistical Alignment Models", Computational Linguistics, volume 29, number 1, pp. 19-51.

Martha Palmer, Daniel Gildea and Paul Kingsbury. 2005. The Proposition Bank: An Annotated Corpus of Semantic Roles. *Computational Linguistics*. Volume 31, Issue 1. pp. 71-106.

Bo Pang, Kevin Knight and Daniel Marcu. 2003. Syntax-based Alignment of Multiple Translations: Extracting Paraphrases and Generating New Sentences. *Proc. HLT/NAACL 2003*.

Fernando Pereira, Naftali Tishby and Lillian Lee. 1993. Distributional Clustering of English Words. *Proc. ACL1993*. pp. 183-190.

Barry Schiffman, Kathleen R. McKeown, Ralph Grishman and James Allan. 2007. Question Answering using Integrated Information Retrieval and Information Extraction. *Proc. HLT-NAACL 2007*. Rochester, US.

Yusuke Shinyama and Satoshi Sekine. 2003. Paraphrase Acquisition for Information Extraction. *Proc. ACL 2003 workshop on Paraphrasing (IWP 2003)*.

Hongye Tan, Tiejun Zhao and Jiaheng Zheng. 2008. Identification of Chinese Event and Their Argument Roles. *Proc. Computer and Information Technology Workshops*.

Nianwen Xue and Martha Palmer. 2009. Adding semantic roles to the Chinese Treebank. *Natural Language Engineering*, 15(1):143-172.

Richard Zens and Hermann Ney. 2004. Improvements in Phrase-Based Statistical Machine Translation. *In HLT/NAACL 2004*. New York City, NY, US

Graph Connectivity Measures for Unsupervised Parameter Tuning of Graph-Based Sense Induction Systems

Ioannis Korkontzelos, Ioannis Klapaftis and Suresh Manandhar
Department of Computer Science
The University of York
Heslington, York, YO10 5NG, UK
{johnkork, giannis, suresh}@cs.york.ac.uk

Abstract

Word Sense Induction (WSI) is the task of identifying the different senses (uses) of a target word in a given text. This paper focuses on the unsupervised estimation of the free parameters of a graph-based WSI method, and explores the use of eight Graph Connectivity Measures (GCM) that assess the degree of connectivity in a graph. Given a target word and a set of parameters, GCM evaluate the connectivity of the produced clusters, which correspond to subgraphs of the initial (unclustered) graph. Each parameter setting is assigned a score according to one of the GCM and the highest scoring setting is then selected. Our evaluation on the nouns of SemEval-2007 WSI task (SWSI) shows that: (1) all GCM estimate a set of parameters which significantly outperform the worst performing parameter setting in both SWSI evaluation schemes, (2) all GCM estimate a set of parameters which outperform the Most Frequent Sense (MFS) baseline by a statistically significant amount in the supervised evaluation scheme, and (3) two of the measures estimate a set of parameters that performs closely to a set of parameters estimated in supervised manner.

1 Introduction

Using word senses instead of word forms is essential in many applications such as information retrieval (IR) and machine translation (MT) (Pantel and Lin, 2002). Word senses are a prerequisite for word sense disambiguation (WSD) algorithms. However, they are usually represented as a fixed-list of definitions of a manually constructed lexical database. The fixed-list of senses paradigm has several disadvantages. Firstly, lexical databases often contain general definitions and miss many domain specific senses (Agirre et al., 2001). Secondly, they suffer from the lack of explicit semantic and topical relations between concepts (Agirre et al., 2001). Thirdly, they often do not reflect the exact content of the context in which the target word appears (Veronis, 2004). WSI aims to overcome these limitations of hand-constructed lexicons.

Most WSI systems are based on the vector-space model that represents each context of a target word as a vector of features (e.g. frequency of cooccurring words). Vectors are clustered and the resulting clusters are taken to represent the induced senses. Recently, graph-based methods have been employed to WSI (Dorow and Widdows, 2003; Veronis, 2004; Agirre and Soroa, 2007b).

Typically, graph-based approaches represent each word co-occurring with the target word, within a pre-specified window, as a vertex. Two vertices are connected via an edge if they co-occur in one or more contexts of the target word. This co-occurrence graph is then clustered employing different graph clustering algorithms to induce the senses. Each cluster (induced sense) consists of words expected to be topically related to the particular sense. As a result, graph-based approaches assume that each context word is related to one and only one sense of the target one.

Recently, Klapaftis and Manandhar (2008) argued that this assumption might not be always valid, since a context word may be related to more than one senses of the target one. As a result, they pro-

Proceedings of the NAACL HLT Workshop on Unsupervised and Minimally Supervised Learning of Lexical Semantics, pages 36–44,
Boulder, Colorado, June 2009.

posed the use of a graph-based model for WSI, in which each vertex of the graph corresponds to a collocation (word-pair) that co-occurs with the target word, while edges are drawn based on the co-occurrence frequency of their associated collocations. Clustering of this collocational graph would produce clusters, which consist of a set of collocations. The intuition is that the produced clusters will be less sense-conflating than those produced by other graph-based approaches, since collocations provide strong and consistent clues to the senses of a target word (Yarowsky, 1995).

The collocational graph-based approach as well as the majority of state-of-the-art WSI systems estimate their parameters either empirically or by employing supervised techniques. The SemEval-2007 WSI task (SWSI) participating systems *UOY* and *UBC-AS* used labeled data for parameter estimation (Agirre and Soroa, 2007a), while the authors of *I2R*, *UPV_SI* and *UMND2* have empirically chosen values for their parameters. This issue imposes limits on the unsupervised nature of these algorithms, as well as on their performance on different datasets.

More specifically, when applying an unsupervised WSI system on different datasets, one cannot be sure that the same set of parameters is appropriate for all datasets (Karakos et al., 2007). In most cases, a new parameter tuning might be necessary. Unsupervised estimation of free parameters may enhance the unsupervised nature of systems, making them applicable to any dataset, even if there are no tagged data available.

In this paper, we focus on estimating the free parameters of the collocational graph-based WSI method (Klapaftis and Manandhar, 2008) using eight graph connectivity measures (GCM). Given a parameter setting and the associated induced clustering solution, each induced cluster corresponds to a subgraph of the original unclustered graph. A graph connectivity measure GCM_i scores each cluster by evaluating the degree of connectivity of its corresponding subgraph. Each clustering solution is then assigned the average of the scores of its clusters. Finally, the highest scoring solution is selected.

Our evaluation on the nouns of SWSI shows that GCM improve the worst performing parameter setting by large margins in both SWSI evaluation schemes, although they are below the best performing parameter setting. Moreover, the evaluation in a WSD setting shows that all GCM estimate a set of parameters which are above the Most Frequent Sense (MFS) baseline by a statistically significant amount. Finally our results show that two of the measures, i.e. average degree and weighted average degree, estimate a set of parameters that performs closely to a set of parameters estimated in a supervised manner. All of these findings, suggest that GCM are able to identify useful differences regarding the quality of the induced clusters for different parameter combinations, in effect being useful for unsupervised parameter estimation.

2 Collocational graphs for WSI

Let bc, be the base corpus, which consists of paragraphs containing the target word tw. The aim is to induce the senses of tw given bc as the only input. Let rc be a large reference corpus. In Klapaftis and Manandhar (2008) the British National Corpus[1] is used as a reference corpus. The WSI algorithm consists of the following stages.

Corpus pre-processing The target of this stage is to filter the paragraphs of the base corpus, in order to keep the words which are topically (and possibly semantically) related to the target one. Initially, tw is removed from bc and both bc and rc are PoS-tagged. In the next step, only nouns are kept in the paragraphs of bc, since they are characterised by higher discriminative ability than verbs, adverbs or adjectives which may appear in a variety of different contexts. At the end of this pre-processing step, each paragraph of bc and rc is a list of lemmatized nouns (Klapaftis and Manandhar, 2008).

In the next step, the paragraphs of bc are filtered by removing common nouns which are noisy; contextually not related to tw. Given a contextual word cw that occurs in the paragraphs of bc, a log-likelihood ratio (G^2) test is employed (Dunning, 1993), which checks if the distribution of cw in bc is similar to the distribution of cw in rc; $p(cw|bc) = p(cw|rc)$ *(null hypothesis)*. If this is true, G^2 has a small value. If this value is less than a pre-specified threshold (parameter p_1) the noun is removed from bc.

[1]The British National Corpus (BNC) (2001, version 2). Distributed by Oxford University Computing Services.

Target: *cnn_nbc*	Target: *nbc_news*
nbc_tv	**nbc_tv**
cnn_tv	soap_opera
cnn_radio	nbc_show
news_newscast	**news_newscast**
radio_television	nbc_newshour
cnn_headline	**cnn_headline**
nbc_politics	radio_tv
breaking_news	**breaking_news**

Table 1: Collocations connected to *cnn_nbc* and *nbc_news*

This process identifies nouns that are more indicative in bc than in rc and vice versa. However, in this setting we are not interested in nouns which have a distinctive frequency in rc. As a result, each cw which has a relative frequency in bc less than in rc is filtered out. At the end of this stage, each paragraph of bc is a list of nouns which are assumed to be contextually related to the target word tw.

Creating the initial collocational graph The target of this stage is to determine the related nouns, which will form the collocations, and the weight of each collocation. Klapaftis and Manandhar (2008) consider collocations of size 2, i.e. pairs of nouns.

For each paragraph of bc of size n, collocations are identified by generating all the possible $\binom{c_n}{2}$ combinations. The frequency of a collocation c is the number of paragraphs in the whole SWSI corpus (27132 paragraphs), in which c occurs.

Each collocation is assigned a weight, measuring the relative frequency of two nouns co-occurring. Let $freq_{ij}$ denote the number of paragraphs in which nouns i and j cooccur, and $freq_j$ denote the number of paragraphs, where noun j occurs. The conditional probability $p(i|j)$ is defined in equation 1, and $p(j|i)$ is computed in a similar way. The weight of collocation c_{ij} is the average of these conditional probabilities $w_{c_{ij}} = p(i|j) + p(j|i)$.

$$p(i|j) = \frac{freq_{ij}}{freq_j} \quad (1)$$

Finally, Klapaftis and Manandhar (2008) only extract collocations which have frequency (parameter p_2) and weight (parameter p_3) higher than prespecified thresholds. This filtering appears to compensate for inaccuracies in G^2, as well as for low-frequency distant collocations that are ambiguous. Each weighted collocation is represented as a vertex. Two vertices share an edge, if they co-occur in one or more paragraphs of bc.

Populating and weighing the collocational graph The constructed graph, G, is sparse, since the previous stage attempted to identify rare events, i.e. co-occurring collocations. To address this problem, Klapaftis and Manandhar (2008) apply a smoothing technique, similar to the one in Cimiano et al. (2005), extending the principle that *a word is characterised by the company it keeps* (Firth, 1957) to collocations. The target is to discover new edges between vertices and to assign weights to all edges.

Each vertex i (collocation c_i) is associated to a vector VC_i containing its neighbouring vertices (collocations). Table 1 shows an example of two vertices, *cnn_nbc* and *nbc_news*, which are disconnected in G of the target word *network*. The example was taken from Klapaftis and Manandhar (2008).

In the next step, the similarity between all vertex vectors VC_i and VC_j is calculated using the Jaccard coefficient, i.e. $JC(VC_i, VC_j) = \frac{|VC_i \cap VC_j|}{|VC_i \cup VC_j|}$. Two collocations c_i and c_j are mutually similar if c_i is the most similar collocation to c_j and vice versa.

Given that collocations c_i and c_j are mutually similar, an occurrence of a collocation c_k with one of c_i, c_j is also counted as an occurrence with the other collocation. For example in Table 1, if *cnn_nbc* and *nbc_news* are mutually similar, then the zero-frequency event between *nbc_news* and *cnn_tv* is set equal to the joint frequency between *cnn_nbc* and *cnn_tv*. Marginal frequencies of collocations are updated and the overall result is consequently a smoothing of relative frequencies.

The weight applied to each edge connecting vertices i and j (collocations c_i and c_j) is the maximum of their conditional probabilities: $p(i|j) = \frac{freq_{ij}}{freq_j}$, where $freq_i$ is the number of paragraphs collocation c_i occurs. $p(j|i)$ is defined similarly.

Inducing senses and tagging In this final stage, the collocational graph is clustered to produced the senses (clusters) of the target word. The clustering method employed is *Chinese Whispers* (CW) (Biemann, 2006). CW is linear to the number of graph edges, while it offers the advantage that it does not require any input parameters, producing the clusters of a graph automatically.

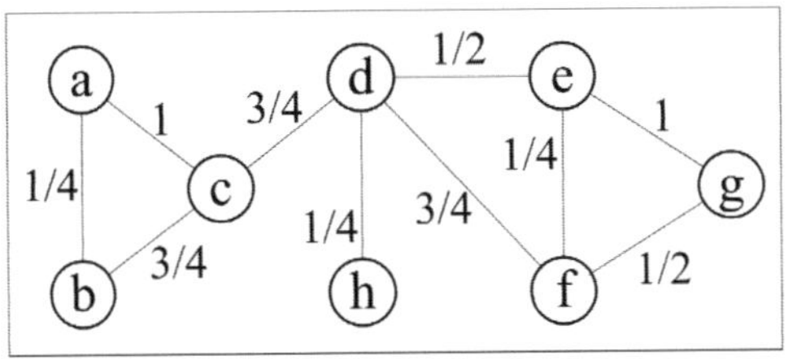

Figure 1: An example undirected weighted graph.

Initially, CW assigns all vertices to different classes. Each vertex i is processed for a number of iterations and inherits the strongest class in its local neighbourhood (LN) in an update step. LN is defined as the set of vertices which share an edge with i. In each iteration for vertex i: each class, cl, receives a score equal to the sum of the weights of edges (i, j), where j has been assigned to class cl. The maximum score determines the strongest class. In case of multiple strongest classes, one is chosen randomly. Classes are updated immediately, meaning that a vertex can inherit from its LN classes that were introduced in the same iteration.

Once CW has produced the clusters of a target word, each of the instances of tw is tagged with one of the induced clusters. This process is similar to Word Sense Disambiguation (WSD) with the difference that the sense repository has been automatically produced. Particularly, given an instance of tw in paragraph p_i: each induced cluster cl is assigned a score equal to the number of its collocations (i.e. pairs of words) occurring in p_i. We observe that the tagging method exploits the one sense per collocation property (Yarowsky, 1995), which means that WSD based on collocations is probably finer than WSD based on simple words, since ambiguity is reduced (Klapaftis and Manandhar, 2008).

3 Unsupervised parameter tuning

In this section we investigate unsupervised ways to address the issue of choosing parameter values. To this end, we employ a variety of GCM, which measure the relative importance of each vertex and assess the overall connectivity of the corresponding graph. These measures are *average degree*, *cluster coefficient*, *graph entropy* and *edge density* (Navigli and Lapata, 2007; Zesch and Gurevych, 2007).

GCM quantify the degree of connectivity of the produced clusters (subgraphs), which represent the senses (uses) of the target word for a given clustering solution (parameter setting). Higher values of GCM indicate subgraphs (clusters) of higher connectivity. Given a parameter setting, the induced clustering solution and a graph connectivity measure GCM_i, each induced cluster is assigned the resulting score of applying GCM_i on the corresponding subgraph of the initial unclustered graph. Each clustering solution is assigned the average of the scores of its clusters (table 6), and the highest scoring one is selected.

For each measure, we have developed two versions, i.e. one which considers the edge weights in the subgraph, and a second which does not. In the following description the terms graph and subgraph are interchangeable.

Let $G = (V, E)$ be an undirected graph (induced sense), where V is a set of vertices and $E = \{(u, v) : u, v \in V\}$ a set of edges connecting vertex pairs. Each edge is weighted by a positive weight, $W : w_{uv} \to [0, \infty)$. Figure 1 shows a small example to explain the computation of GCM. The graph consists of 8 vertices, $|V| = 8$, and 10 edges, $|E| = 10$. Edge weights appear on edges, e.g. $w_{ab} = \frac{1}{4}$.

Average Degree The *degree (deg)* of a vertex u is the number of edges connected to u:

$$deg(u) = |\{(u, v) \in E : v \in V\}| \quad (2)$$

The *average degree (AvgDeg)* of a graph can be computed as:

$$AvgDeg(G(V, E)) = \frac{1}{|V|} \sum_{u \in V} deg(u) \quad (3)$$

The first row of table 2 shows the vertex degrees of the example graph (figure 1) and $AvgDeg(G) = \frac{20}{8} = 2.5$.

Edge weights can be integrated into the degree computation. Let mew be the maximum edge weight in the graph:

$$mew = \max_{(u,v) \in E} w_{uv} \quad (4)$$

Average Weighted Degree The *weighted degree(w_deg)* of a vertex is defined as:

$$w\_deg(u) = \frac{1}{|V|} \sum_{(u,v) \in E} \frac{w_{uv}}{mew} \quad (5)$$

	a	b	c	d	e	f	g	h
$deg(u)$	2	2	3	4	3	3	2	1
$wdeg(u)$	$\frac{5}{4}$	1	$\frac{5}{2}$	$\frac{9}{4}$	$\frac{7}{4}$	$\frac{3}{2}$	$\frac{3}{2}$	$\frac{1}{4}$
T_u	1	1	1	1	1	2	1	0
$cc(u)$	1	1	$\frac{1}{3}$	$\frac{1}{6}$	$\frac{1}{3}$	$\frac{2}{3}$	1	0
WT_u	$\frac{3}{4}$	1	$\frac{1}{4}$	$\frac{1}{4}$	$\frac{1}{2}$	$\frac{3}{2}$	$\frac{1}{4}$	0
$wcc(u)$	$\frac{3}{4}$	1	$\frac{1}{12}$	$\frac{1}{24}$	$\frac{1}{6}$	$\frac{1}{2}$	$\frac{1}{4}$	0
$p(u)$	$\frac{1}{10}$	$\frac{1}{10}$	$\frac{3}{20}$	$\frac{1}{5}$	$\frac{3}{20}$	$\frac{3}{20}$	$\frac{1}{10}$	$\frac{1}{20}$
$en(u) * 100$	33	33	41	46	41	41	33	22
$wp(u)$	$\frac{1}{16}$	$\frac{1}{20}$	$\frac{1}{8}$	$\frac{9}{80}$	$\frac{7}{80}$	$\frac{3}{40}$	$\frac{3}{40}$	$\frac{1}{80}$
$we(u) * 100$	25	22	38	35	31	28	28	8

Table 2: Computations of graph connectivity measures and relevant quantities on the example graph (figure 1).

Average weighted degree (AvgWDeg), similarly to *AvgDeg*, is averaged over all vertices of the graph. In the graph of figure 1, $mew = 1$. The second row of table 2 shows the weighted degrees of all vertices. $AvgWDeg(G) = \frac{48}{36} \simeq 1.33$.

Average Cluster Coefficient The *cluster coefficient (cc)* of a vertex, u, is defined as:

$$cc(u) = \frac{T_u}{2^{-1}k_u(k_u - 1)} \quad (6)$$

$$T_u = \sum_{(u,v)\in E} \sum_{\substack{(v,x)\in E \\ x\neq u}} 1 \quad (7)$$

T_u is the number of edges between the k_u neighbours of u. Obviously $k_u = deg(u)$. $2^{-1}k_u(k_u - 1)$ would be the number of edges between the neighbours of u if the graph they define was fully connected. *Average cluster coefficient (AvgCC)* is averaged over all vertices of the graph.

The computations of T_u and $cc(u)$ on the example graph are shown in the third and fourth rows of table 2. Consequently, $AvgCC(G) = \frac{9}{16} = 0.5625$.

Average Weighted Cluster Coefficient Let WT_u be the sum of edge weights between the neighbours of u over mew. *Weighted cluster coefficient (wcc)* can be computed as:

$$wcc(u) = \frac{WT_u}{2^{-1}k_u(k_u - 1)} \quad (8)$$

$$WT_u = \frac{1}{mew} \sum_{(u,v)\in E} \sum_{\substack{(v,x)\in E \\ x\neq u}} w_{vx} \quad (9)$$

Average weighted cluster coefficient (AvgWCC) is averaged over all vertices of the graph. The computations of WT_u and $wcc(u)$ on the example graph (figure 1) are shown in the fifth and sixth rows of table 2 and $AvgWCC(G) = \frac{67}{8*24} \simeq 0.349$.

Graph Entropy *Entropy* measures the amount of information (alternatively the uncertainty) in a random variable. For a graph, high *entropy* indicates that many vertices are equally important and low *entropy* that only few vertices are relevant (Navigli and Lapata, 2007). The *entropy (en)* of a vertex u can be defined as:

$$en(u) = -p(u)\log_2 p(u) \quad (10)$$

The probability of a vertex, $p(u)$, is determined by the degree distribution:

$$p(u) = \left\{\frac{deg(u)}{2|E|}\right\}_{u\in V} \quad (11)$$

Graph entropy (GE) is computed by summing all vertex entropies and normalising by $\log_2 |V|$. The seventh and eighth row of table 2 show the computations of $p(u)$ and $en(u)$ on the example graph, respectively. Thus, $GE \simeq 0.97$.

Weighted Graph Entropy Similarly to previous *graph connectivity* measures, the *weighted entropy (wen)* of a vertex u is defined as:

$$we(u) = -wp(u)\log_2 wp(u) \quad (12)$$

$$\text{where: } wp(u) = \left\{\frac{w\_deg(u)}{2 * mew * |E|}\right\}_{u\in V}$$

Weighted graph entropy (GE) is computed by summing all vertex weighted entropies and normalising by $\log_2 |V|$. The last two rows of table 2 show the computations of $wp(u)$ and $we(u)$ on the example graph. Consequently, $WGE \simeq 0.73$.

Edge Density and Weighted Edge Density *Edge density (ed)* quantifies how many edges the graph has, as a ratio over the number of edges of a fully connected graph of the same size:

$$A(V) = 2\binom{|V|}{2} \quad (13)$$

Edge density (ed) is a global graph connectivity measure; it refers to the whole graph and not a specific vertex. *Edge density (ed)* and *weighted edge density (wed)* can be defined as follows:

$$ed(G(V,E)) = \frac{|E|}{A(V)} \quad (14)$$

$$wed(G(V,E)) = \frac{1}{A(V)} \sum_{(u,v)\in E} \frac{w_{u,v}}{mew} \quad (15)$$

In the graph of figure 1: $A(V) = 2\binom{8}{2} = 28$, $ed(G) = \frac{10}{28} \simeq 0.357$, $\sum \frac{w_{u,v}}{mew} = 6$ and $wed(G) = \frac{6}{28} \simeq 0.214$.

The use of the aforementioned GCM allows the estimation of a different parameter setting for each target word. Table 3 shows the parameters of the collocational graph-based WSI system (Klapaftis and Manandhar, 2008). These parameters affect how the collocational graph is constructed, and in effect the quality of the induced clusters.

4 Evaluation

4.1 Experimental setting

The collocational WSI approach was evaluated under the framework and corpus of SemEval-2007 WSI task (Agirre and Soroa, 2007a). The corpus consists of text of the Wall Street Journal corpus, and is hand-tagged with OntoNotes senses (Hovy et al., 2006). The evaluation focuses on all 35 nouns of SWSI. SWSI task employs two evaluation schemes. In *unsupervised evaluation*, the results are treated as clusters of contexts and gold standard (GS) senses as classes. In a perfect clustering solution, each induced cluster contains the same contexts as one of the classes (*Homogeneity*), and each class contains the same contexts as one of the clusters (*Completeness*). F-Score is used to assess the overall quality of clustering. Entropy and purity are also used, complementarily. F-Score is a better measure than entropy or purity, since F-Score measures both homogeneity and completeness, while entropy and purity measure only the former. In the second scheme, *supervised evaluation*, the training corpus is used to map the induced clusters to GS senses. The testing corpus is then used to measure WSD performance (Table 4, *Sup. Recall*).

The graph-based collocational WSI method is referred as *Col-Sm* (where "Col" stands for the "collocational WSI" approach and "Sm" for its version using "smoothing"). *Col-Bl* (where "Bl" stands for "baseline") refers to the same system without smoothing. The parameters of *Col-Sm* were originally estimated by cross-validation on the training set of SWSI. Out of 72 parameter combinations, the setting with the highest F-Score was chosen and applied to all 35 nouns of the test set. This is referred as *Col-Sm-org* (where "org" stands for "original") in Table 4. Table 3 shows all values for each parameter, and the chosen values, under supervised parameter estimation[2]. *Col-Bl-org* (Table 4) induces senses as *Col-Sm-org* does, but without smoothing.

Parameter	Range	Value
G^2 threshold	5, 10, 15	$p_1 = 5$
Collocation frequency	4, 6, 8, 10	$p_2 = 8$
Collocation weight	0.2, 0.3, 0.4	$p_3 = 0.2$

Table 3: Parameters ranges and values in Klapaftis and Manandhar (2008)

In table 4, *Col-Sm-w* (respectively *Col-Bl-w*) refers to the evaluation of *Col-Sm* (*Col-Bl*), following the same technique for parameter estimation as in Klapaftis and Manandhar (2008) for each target word separately ("w" stands for "word"). Given that GCM are applied for each target word separately, these baselines will allow to see the performance of GCM compared to a supervised setting.

The 1c1inst baseline assigns each instance to a distinct cluster, while the 1c1w baseline groups all instances of a target word into a single cluster. 1c1w is equivalent to MFS in this setting. The fifth column of table 4 shows the average number of clusters.

The SWSI participant systems *UOY* and *UBC-AS* used labeled data for parameter estimation. The authors of *I2R*, *UPV_SI* and *UMND2* have empirically chosen values for their parameters.

The next subsection presents the evaluation of GCM as well as the results of SWSI systems. Initially, we provide a brief discussion on the differences between the two evaluation schemes of SWSI that will allow for a better understanding of GCM performance.

4.2 Analysis of results and discussion

Evaluation of WSI methods is a difficult task. For instance, *1c1inst* (Table 4) achieves perfect purity

[2]CW performed 200 iterations for all experiments, because it is not guaranteed to converge.

System	Unsupervised Evaluation				Sup.
	FSc.	Pur.	Ent.	# Cl.	Recall
Col-Sm-org	78.0	88.6	31.0	5.9	86.4
Col-Bl-org	73.1	89.6	29.0	8.0	85.6
Col-Sm-w	80.9	88.0	32.5	4.3	85.5
Col-Bl-w	78.1	88.3	31.7	5.4	84.3
UBC-AS	80.8	83.6	43.5	1.6	80.7
UPV_SI	69.9	87.4	30.9	7.2	82.5
I2R	68.0	88.4	29.7	3.1	86.8
UMND2	67.1	85.8	37.6	1.7	84.5
UOY	65.8	89.8	25.5	11.3	81.6
1c1w-MFS	80.7	82.4	46.3	1	80.9
1c1inst	6.6	100	0	73.1	N/A

Table 4: Evaluation of WSI systems and baselines.

System	Bound type	Unsupervised Evaluation				Sup. Recall
		FSc.	Pur.	Ent.	# Cl.	
Col-Sm	MaxR	79.3	90.5	26.6	7.0	**88.6**
Col-Sm	MinR	62.9	89.0	26.7	12.7	**78.8**
Col-Bl	MaxR	72.9	91.8	23.2	9.6	**88.7**
Col-Bl	MinR	57.5	89.0	26.4	14.4	**76.2**
Col-Sm	MaxF	**83.2**	90.0	28.7	4.9	86.6
Col-Sm	MinF	**43.6**	90.2	22.1	17.6	83.7
Col-Bl	MaxF	**81.1**	90.0	28.7	5.3	81.8
Col-Bl	MinF	**34.1**	90.5	20.5	20.4	81.5

Table 5: Upper and lower performance bounds for systems *Col-Sm* and *Col-Bl*.

and entropy. However, F-Score of *1clinst* is low, because the GS senses are spread among clusters, decreasing unsupervised recall. Supervised recall of *1clinst* is undefined, because each cluster tags only one instance. Hence, clusters tagging instances in the test corpus do not tag any instances in the train corpus and the mapping cannot be performed. *1clw* achieves high F-Score due to the dominance of MFS in the testing corpus. However, its purity, entropy and supervised recall are much lower than other systems, because it only induces the dominant sense.

Clustering solutions that achieve high supervised recall do not necessarily achieve high F-Score, mainly because F-Score penalises systems for inducing more clusters than the corresponding GS classes, as *1cl1inst* does. Supervised evaluation seems to be more neutral regarding the number of clusters, since clusters are mapped into a weighted vector of senses. Thus, inducing a number of clusters similar to the number of senses is not a requirement for good results (Agirre and Soroa, 2007a). High supervised recall means high purity and entropy, as in *I2R*, but not vice versa, as in *UOY*. *UOY* produces many clean clusters, however these are unreliably mapped to senses due to insufficient training data. On the contrary, *I2R* produces a few clean clusters, which are mapped more reliably.

Comparing the performance of SWSI systems shows that none performs well in both evaluation settings, in effect being biased against one of the schemes. However, this is not the case for the collocational WSI method, which achieves a high performance in both evaluation settings.

Table 6 presents the results of applying the graph connectivity measures of section 3 in order to choose the parameter values for the collocational WSI system, for each word separately. The evaluation is done both for *Col-Sm* and *Col-Bl* that use and ignore smoothing, respectively.

To evaluate the supervised recall performance using the graph connectivity measures, we computed both the upper and lower bounds of *Col-Sm*, i.e. the best and worst supervised recall, respectively (MaxR and MinR in table 5). In the former case, we selected the parameter combination per target word that performs best (Col-Sm, MaxR in table 5), which resulted in 88.6% supervised recall (F-Score: 79.3%), while in the latter we selected the worst performing one, which resulted in 78.8% supervised recall (F-Score: 62.9%). In table 6 we observe that the supervised recall of all measures is significantly lower than the upper bound. However, all measures perform significantly better than the lower bound (McNemar's test, confidence level: 95%); the smallest difference is 4.9%, in the case of weighted edge density. The picture is the same for *Col-Bl*.

In the same vein, we computed both the upper and lower bounds of *Col-Sm* in terms of F-Score, 83.2% and 43.6%, respectively (Col-Sm, MinF and MaxF in table 5). The performance of the system is lower than the upper bound, for all GCM. Despite that, we observe that all measures except edge density and weighted edge density outperform the lower bound by large margins.

The comparison of GCM performance against the lower and upper bounds of *Col-Sm* and *Col-Bl* shows that GCM are able to identify useful differences regarding the degree of connectivity of induced clusters, and in effect suggest parameter values that perform significantly better than the worst

	Col-Sm					Col-Bl				
	Unsupervised Evaluation				Sup.	Unsupervised Evaluation				Sup.
Graph Connectivity Measure	FSc	Pur.	Ent.	# Cl.	Recall	FSc	Pur.	Ent.	# Cl.	Recall
Average Degree	**79.2**	87.2	34.2	3.9	**84.8**	**77.5**	31.3	88.4	5.7	**83.8**
Average Weighted Degree	77.1	87.8	32.0	5.5	84.2	75.1	28.3	89.6	8.5	83.3
Average Cluster Coefficient	72.5	88.8	28.5	9.1	83.9	68.7	24.0	90.9	12.9	83.9
Average Weighted Cluster Coefficient	65.8	88.4	28.0	9.6	84.1	68.9	22.4	91.3	13.9	83.7
Graph Entropy	67.0	89.6	25.9	12.3	83.8	68.5	22.1	91.8	14.4	**84.4**
Weighted Graph Entropy	72.7	89.4	28.1	9.6	84.1	72.2	23.5	91.2	12.5	84.0
Edge Density	47.8	91.8	19.4	18.4	**84.8**	42.0	16.9	92.8	21.9	84.1
Weighted Edge Density	53.4	90.2	23.1	15.5	83.7	42.2	17.1	92.7	21.9	83.9

Table 6: Unsupervised & supervised evaluation of the collocational WSI approach using graph connectivity measures.

case. However, they are all unable to approximate the upper bound for both evaluation schemes, which is also the case for the supervised estimation of parameters per target word (*Col-Sm-w* and *Col-Bl-w*).

In Table 6, we also observe that all measures achieve higher supervised recall scores than the MFS baseline. The increase is statistically significant (McNemar's test, confidence level: 95%) in all cases. This result shows that irrespective of the number of clusters produced (low F-Score), GCM are able to estimate a set of parameters that provides clean clusters (low entropy), which when mapped to GS senses improve upon the most frequent heuristic, unlike the majority of unsupervised WSD systems.

Regarding the comparison between different GCM, we observe that average degree and weighted average degree for *Col-Sm* (*Col-Bl*) perform closely to *Col-Sm-w* (*Col-Bl-w*) for both evaluation schemes. This is due to the fact that they produce a number of clusters similar to *Col-Sm-w* (*Col-Bl-w*), while at the same time their distributions of clusters over the target words' instances are also similar.

On the contrary, the remaining GCM tend to produce larger numbers of clusters compared to both *Col-Sm-w* (*Col-Bl-w*) and the GS, in effect being penalised by F-Score. As it has already been mentioned, supervised recall is less affected by a large number of clusters, which causes small differences among GCM.

Determining whether the weighted or unweighted version of GCM performs better depends on the GCM itself. Weighted graph entropy performs in all cases better than the unweighted version. For average cluster coefficient and edge density, we cannot extract a safe conclusion. Unweighted average degree performs better than the weighted version.

5 Conclusion and future work

In this paper, we explored the use of eight graph connectivity measures for unsupervised estimation of free parameters of a collocational graph-based WSI system. Given a parameter setting and the associated induced clustering solution, each cluster was scored according to the connectivity degree of its corresponding subgraph, as assessed by a particular graph connectivity measure. Each clustering solution was then assigned the average of its clusters' scores, and the highest scoring one was selected.

Evaluation on the nouns of SemEval-2007 WSI task (SWSI) showed that all eight graph connectivity measures choose parameters for which the corresponding performance of the system is significantly higher than the lower performance bound, for both the supervised and unsupervised evaluation scheme. Moreover, the selected parameters produce results which outperform the MFS baseline by a statistically significant amount in the supervised evaluation scheme. The best performing measures, average degree and weighted average degree, perform comparably well to the set of parameters chosen by a supervised parameter estimation. In general, graph connectivity measures can quantify significant differences regarding the degree of connectivity of induced clusters.

Future work focuses on further exploiting graph connectivity measures. Graph theoretic literature proposes a variety of measures capturing graph properties. Some of these measures might help in improving WSI performance, while at the same time keeping graph-based WSI systems totally unsupervised.

References

Eneko Agirre and Aitor Soroa. 2007a. Semeval-2007 task 02: Evaluating word sense induction and discrimination systems. In *Proceedings of the Fourth International Workshop on Semantic Evaluations (SemEval-2007)*, pages 7–12, Prague, Czech Republic. Association for Computational Linguistics.

Eneko Agirre and Aitor Soroa. 2007b. Ubc-as: A graph based unsupervised system for induction and classification. In *Proceedings of the Fourth International Workshop on Semantic Evaluations (SemEval-2007)*, pages 346–349, Prague, Czech Republic. Association for Computational Linguistics.

Eneko Agirre, Olatz Ansa, Eduard Hovy, and David Martinez. 2001. Enriching wordnet concepts with topic signatures, Sep.

Chris Biemann. 2006. Chinese whispers - an efficient graph clustering algorithm and its application to natural language processing problems. In *Proceedings of TextGraphs: the Second Workshop on Graph Based Methods for Natural Language Processing*, pages 73–80, New York City, June. Association for Computational Linguistics.

Philipp Cimiano, Andreas Hotho, and Steffen Staab. 2005. Learning concept hierarchies from text corpora using formal concept analysis. *Journal of Artificial Intelligence research*, 24:305–339.

Beate Dorow and Dominic Widdows. 2003. Discovering corpusspecific word senses. In *Proceedings 10th conference of the European chapter of the ACL*, pages 79–82, Budapest, Hungary.

Ted E. Dunning. 1993. Accurate methods for the statistics of surprise and coincidence. *Computational Linguistics*, 19(1):61–74.

John R. Firth. 1957. A synopsis of linguistic theory, 1930-1955. *Studies in Linguistic Analysis*, pages 1–32.

Eduard Hovy, Mitchell Marcus, Martha Palmer, Lance Ramshaw, and Ralph Weischedel. 2006. Ontonotes: The 90% solution. In *Proceedings of the Human Language Technology Conference of the NAACL, Companion Volume: Short Papers*, pages 57–60, New York City, USA. Association for Computational Linguistics.

Damianos Karakos, Jason Eisner, Sanjeev Khudanpur, and Carey Priebe. 2007. Cross-instance tuning of unsupervised document clustering algorithms. In *Human Language Technologies 2007: The Conference of the North American Chapter of the Association for Computational Linguistics; Proceedings of the Main Conference*, pages 252–259, Rochester, New York, April. Association for Computational Linguistics.

Ioannis P. Klapaftis and Suresh Manandhar. 2008. Word sense induction using graphs of collocations. In *In Proceedings of the 18th European Conference on Artificial Intelligence, (ECAI-2008)*, Patras, Greece.

R. Navigli and M. Lapata. 2007. Graph connectivity measures for unsupervised word sense disambiguation. In *20th International Joint Conference on Artificial Intelligence (IJCAI 2007)*, pages 1683–1688, Hyderabad, India, January.

Patrick Pantel and Dekang Lin. 2002. Discovering word senses from text. In *KDD '02: Proceedings of the eighth ACM SIGKDD international conference on Knowledge discovery and data mining*, pages 613–619, New York, NY, USA. ACM Press.

Jean Veronis. 2004. Hyperlex: lexical cartography for information retrieval. *Computer Speech & Language*, 18(3):223–252, July.

David Yarowsky. 1995. Unsupervised word sense disambiguation rivaling supervised methods. In *Meeting of the Association for Computational Linguistics*, pages 189–196.

Torsten Zesch and Iryna Gurevych. 2007. Analysis of the wikipedia category graph for NLP applications. In *Proceedings of the Second Workshop on TextGraphs: Graph-Based Algorithms for Natural Language Processing*, pages 1–8, Rochester, NY, USA. Association for Computational Linguistics.

Combining Syntactic Co-occurrences and Nearest Neighbours in Distributional Methods to Remedy Data Sparseness.

Lonneke van der Plas
Department of Linguistics
University of Geneva
Geneva, Switzerland

Abstract

The task of automatically acquiring semantically related words have led people to study distributional similarity. The distributional hypothesis states that words that are similar share similar contexts. In this paper we present a technique that aims at improving the performance of a syntax-based distributional method by augmenting the original input of the system (syntactic co-occurrences) with the output of the system (nearest neighbours). This technique is based on the idea of the transitivity of similarity.

1 Introduction

The approach described in this paper builds on the DISTRIBUTIONAL HYPOTHESIS, the idea that semantically related words are distributed similarly over contexts. Harris (1968) claims that, 'the meaning of entities and the meaning of grammatical relations among them, is related to the restriction of combinations of these entities relative to other entities.' In other words, you can grasp the meaning of a word by looking at its context.

Context can be defined in many ways. In this paper we look at the syntactic contexts a word is found in. For example, the verbs that are in a object relation with a particular noun form a part of its context. In accordance with the Firthian tradition these contexts can be used to determine the semantic relatedness of words. For instance, words that occur in a object relation with the verb *drink* have something in common: they are liquid. We will refer to words linked by a syntactic relation, such as *drink -OBJ- beer*, as SYNTACTIC CO-OCCURRENCES. Syntactic co-occurrences have often been used in work on lexical acquisition (Lin, 1998b; Dagan et al., 1999; Curran and Moens, 2002; Alfonseca and Manandhar, 2002).

Distributional methods for automatic acquisition of semantically related words suffer from data sparseness. They generally perform less well on low-frequency words (Weeds and Weir, 2005; van der Plas, 2008). This is a pity because the available resources for semantically related words usually cover the frequent words rather well. It is for the low-frequency words that automatic methods would be most welcome.

This paper tries to find a way to improve the performance on the words that are most wanted: the middle to very-low-frequency words. At the basis of the proposed technique lies the intuition that semantic similarity between concepts is transitive: if A is like B and B is like C $\rightarrow$ A is like C. As explained in the second paragraph of this section, the fact that both *milk* and *water* are found in object relation with the verb *to drink* tells us that they might be similar. However, even if we had never seen *lemonade* in the same syntactic contexts as *water*, we could still infer that *lemonade* and *water* are similar because we have found evidence that both *water* and *lemonade* are similar to *milk*.

In an ideal world we would be able to infer that *milk* and *water* are related from the syntactic co-occurrences alone, however, because of data sparseness we might not always encounter this evidence directly. We hope that nearest neighbours are able to account for the missing information. Nearest neighbours such as *milk* and *water*, and *water* and *lemonade* are the output of our system. We used the nearest neighbours (the output of our system) as input to our system that normally takes syntactic co-

Proceedings of the NAACL HLT Workshop on Unsupervised and Minimally Supervised Learning of Lexical Semantics, pages 45–53,
Boulder, Colorado, June 2009. ©2009 Association for Computational Linguistics

occurrences as input. Thus it uses the output of the system as input in a second round to smooth the syntactic co-occurrences.

Grefenstette (1994) discusses the difference between FIRST- AND SECOND-ORDER AFFINITIES. There exists a first-order affinity between words if they often appear in the same context, i.e., if they are often found in the vicinity of each other. Words that co-occur frequently such as *orange* and *squeezed* have a first-order affinity. There exists a second-order affinity between words if they share many first-order affinities. These words need not appear together themselves, but their contexts are similar. *Orange* and *lemon* appear often in similar contexts such as being the object of *squeezed*, or being modified by *juicy*.

In this paper we will use second-order affinities as input to the distributional system. We are thus computing THIRD-ORDER AFFINITIES.[1] There exists a third-order affinity between words, if they share many second-order affinities. If *pear* and *watermelon* are similar and *orange* and *watermelon* are similar, then *pear* and *orange* have a third-order affinity.

We will refer to traditional approaches that compute second-order affinities as second-order techniques. In this paper we will compare a second-order technique with a third-order technique, a technique that computes third-order affinities. In addition we use a combined technique that combines both second-order and third-order techniques.

2 Previous work

In Edmonds (1997) the term third-order is used to refer to a different concept. Firstly, we have to mention that the author is working in a proximity-based framework, that is, he is concerned with co-occurrences of words in text, not relations between words in syntactic dependencies. Secondly, the notion of higher-order co-occurrences refers to connectivity paths in networks, i.e. the network of relations between words co-occurring is augmented by connecting words that are connected by a path of length 2 (second-order co-occurrences) and paths of length 3 (third-order co-occurrences) and so on. In the above example *water* and *lemonade* would be connected by a second-order relation implied by the network in which *water* and *lemonade* both co-occur with for example *to pour*. A third-order relation would be implied between *lemonade* and *drink* if *drink* should co-occur with *water*. We define third-order affinity as an iterative process of calculating similarity. The output of the system is fed into the system again. There exists a third-order affinity between words if they share many nearest neighbours with another word, not if a word shares a context that in turn shares a context with the other word. The same perspective on higher-order co-occurrence, that of connectivity paths in networks, is taken in literature of computational modelling of the acquisition of word meaning (Lemaire and Denhire, 2006).

Although Biemann et al. (2004) work in the same proximity-based tradition as the previous authors their notion of third-order is closer to our definition. It is defined as an iterative process in which words are linked when their co-occurrence score trespasses a certain threshold. These nth-order co-occurrences are then used to construct an artificial corpus consisting of the co-occurrence sets retrieved from the original corpus.

Schütze and Walsh (2008) present a graph-theoretic model of lexical-syntactic representation in which higher-order syntactic relations, those that require some generalisation, are defined recursively. The problem they are trying to solve, lexical syntactic acquisition, is different form ours and so is the evaluation method: discriminating sentences that exhibit local coherence from those that do not. Again the method is proximity-based, but since the context are defined very locally (left and right neighbours) the results are likely to be more comparable to a syntax-based method than proximity-based methods that use larger contexts.

3 Limits of the transitivity of similarity

The validity of the third-order affinities is dependent on the transitivity of the similarity between concepts. Unfortunately, it is not always the case that the similarity between A and B and B and C implies the similarity between A and C.

[1] Grefenstette (1994) uses the term third-order affinities for a different concept, i.e. for the subgroupings that can be found in list of second-order nearest neighbours.

When two concepts are identical, the transitivity of similarity holds. If A=B AND B=C → A=C. Does the same reasoning hold for similarity of a lesser degree? For (near-)synonyms the transitivity holds and it is symmetric. If *felicity* is like *gladness*, and *gladness* is like *joy* → *felicity* is like *joy*. Also, the near-synonymy relation is symmetric. We can infer that *gladness* is like *felicity*.

Tversky and Gati (1978) give an example of co-hyponymy where transitivity does not hold. Jamaica is similar to Cuba (with respect to geographical proximity); Cuba is similar to Russia (with respect to their political affinity), but Jamaica and Russia are not similar at all. Geographical proximity and political affinity are SEPARABLE FEATURES. *Cuba* and *Jamaica* are co-hyponyms if we imagine a hypernym *Caribbean islands* of which both concepts are daughters. *Cuba* and *Russia* are co-hyponyms too, but being daughters of another mother, i.e. the concept *communist countries*. The concept *Jamaica* thus inherits features from multiple mothers. What can we say about the transitivity of meaning in this case? The transitivity between two co-hyponyms holds when restricted to single inheritance.

When words are ambiguous, we come to a similar situation. Widdows (2004) gives the following example: *Apple* is similar to *IBM* in the domain of computer companies; *Apple* is similar to *pear*, when we are thinking of fruit. *Pear* and *IBM* are not similar at all. Again, there is the problem of multiple inheritance. *Apple* is a daughter both of the concept *computer manufacturers* and of *fruits*. For co-hyponyms similarity is only transitive in case of single inheritance. The same holds for synonyms. If a word has multiple senses we get into trouble when applying the transitivity of meaning.

Although we have seen many examples of cases where the transitivity of meaning does not hold, we hope to find improvements for finding semantically related words, when using third-order affinity techniques.

4 Methodology

We will now describe the methodology used to compute nearest neighbours (subsection 4.1). In subsection 4.2 we will describe how we have used these nearest neighbours as input to the third-order and combined technique.

4.1 Syntax-based distributional similarity

In this section we will describe the syntactic contexts selected, the data we used, and the measures and weights applied to retrieve nearest neighbours.

4.1.1 Syntactic context

Most research has been done using a limited number of syntactic relations (Lee, 1999; Weeds, 2003). We use several syntactic relations: subject, object, adjective, coordination, apposition, and prepositional complement. In Figure 1 examples are given for these types of syntactic relations.[2]

Subj:	`De` *`kat eet`*`.` 'The cat eats.'
Obj:	`Ik` *`voer`* `de` *`kat`*`.` 'I feed the cat.'
Adj:	`De` *`langharige kat`* `loopt.` 'The long-haired cat walks.'
Coord:	*`Jip and Janneke`* `spelen.` 'Jip and Janneke are playing.'
Appo:	`De` *`clown Bassie`* `lacht.` 'The clown Bassie is laughing.'
Prep:	`Ik` *`begin met`* `mijn` *`werk`*`.` 'I start with my work.'

Figure 1: Types of syntactic relations extracted

4.1.2 Data collection

Because we believe that the method will remedy data sparseness we applied the method to a medium-sized corpus. Approximately 80 million words of Dutch newspaper text.[3] All data is parsed automatically using the Alpino parser (van Noord, 2006). The result of parsing a sentence is a dependency graph according to the guidelines of the Corpus of Spoken Dutch (Moortgat et al., 2000).

4.1.3 Syntactic co-occurrences

For each noun we find its syntactic contexts in the data. This results in CO-OCCURRENCE VECTORS, such as the vector given in Table 1 for the headword *kat*. These are used to find distributionally similar

[2]We are working on Dutch and we are thus dealing with Dutch data.

[3]This is the so-called CLEF corpus as it was used in the Cross Language Evaluation Forum (CLEF). The corpus is a subset of the TwNC corpus (Ordelman, 2002).

	heb_OBJ 'have_OBJ'	voer_OBJ 'feed_OBJ'	harig_ADJ 'furry'_ADJ'
kat 'cat'	50	10	25

Table 1: Syntactic co-occurrence vector for *kat*

words. Every cell in the vector refers to a particular SYNTACTIC CO-OCCURRENCE TYPE, for example, *kat* 'cat' in object relation with *voer* 'feed'. The values of these cells indicate the number of times the co-occurrence type under consideration is found in the corpus. In the example, *kat* 'cat' is found in object relation with *voer* 'feed' 10 times. In other words, the CELL FREQUENCY for this co-occurrence type is 10.

The first column of this table shows the HEADWORD, i.e. the word for which we determine the contexts it is found in. Here, we only find *kat* 'cat'. The first row shows the contexts that are found, i.e. the syntactic relation plus the accompanying word. These contexts are referred to by the terms FEATURES or ATTRIBUTES.

Each co-occurrence type has a cell frequency. Likewise each headword has a ROW FREQUENCY. The row frequency of a certain headword is the sum of all its cell frequencies. In our example the row frequency for the word *kat* 'cat' is 85. Cut-offs for cell and row frequency can be applied to discard certain infrequent co-occurrence types or headwords, respectively. We use cutoffs because we have too little confidence in our characterisations of words with low frequency. We have set a row cut-off of 10. So only headwords that appear in 10 or more co-occurrence tokens in total are taken into account. We have not set a cutoff for the cell frequency.

4.1.4 Measures and feature weights

Some syntactic contexts are more informative than others. Large frequency counts do not always indicate an important syntactic co-occurrence. A large number of nouns can occur as the subject of the verb *hebben* 'have'. The verb *hebben* is selectionally weak (Resnik, 1993) or a LIGHT verb. A verb such as *voer* 'feed' on the other hand occurs much less frequently, and only with a restricted set of nouns as direct object. Intuitively, the fact that two nouns both occur as subject of *hebben* tells us less about their semantic similarity than the fact that two nouns both occur as the direct object of *feed*. The results of vector-based methods can be improved if we take into account the fact that not all combinations of a word and syntactic relation have the same information value. We have used POINTWISE MUTUAL INFORMATION (PMI, Church and Hanks (1989)) to account for the differences in information value between the several headwords and attributes.

The more similar the co-occurrence vectors of any two headwords are, the more distributionally similar the headwords are. In order to compare the vectors of any two headwords, we need a similarity measure. In these experiments we have used a variant of Dice: Dice†, proposed by Curran and Moens (2002). It is defined as:

$$Dice\dagger = \frac{2\sum min(wgt(W1, *_r, *_{w'}), wgt(W2, *_r, *_{w'}))}{\sum wgt(W1, *_r, *_{w'}) + wgt(W2, *_r, *_{w'})}$$

We describe the function using an extension of the notation used by Lin (1998a), adapted by Curran (2003). Co-occurrence data is described as relation tuples: ⟨word, relation, word′⟩, for example, ⟨cat, obj, have⟩.

Asterisks indicate a set of values ranging over all existing values of that component of the relation tuple. For example, $(w, *, *)$ denotes for a given word w all relations with any other word it has been found in. $W1$ and $W2$ are the two words we are comparing, and wgt is the weight given by PMI.

Whereas Dice does not take feature weights into account, Dice† does. For each feature two words share, the minimum is taken. If $W1$ occurred 15 times with relation r and word w' and $W2$ occurred 10 times with relation r and word w', it selects 10 as the minimum (if weighting is set to 1). Note that Dice† gives the same ranking as the well-known Jaccard measure, i.e. there is a monotonic transformation between their scores. Dice† is easier to compute and therefore the preferred measure (Curran and Moens, 2002). Choices for measures and weights are based on previous work (van der Plas and Bouma, 2005).

4.2 Syntactic co-occurrences and nearest neighbours

The syntactic co-occurrence vectors have co-occurrence frequencies as values. An example is given in Figure 2.

GRACHT 'canal'		
97	Amsterdams_ADJ	'Amsterdam_ADJ'
26	ben_SUBJ	'am_SUBJ'
12	word_SUBJ	'become_SUBJ'
9	straat_CONJ	'street_CONJ'
9	gedempt_ADJ	'closed_ADJ'
8	Utrechts_ADJ	Utrecht_ADJ
5	wal_CONJ	'shore_CONJ'
5	muur_CONJ	'wall_CONJ'
5	moet_SUBJ	'has to_SUBJ'
5	graaf_OBJ	'ditch_OBJ'

Figure 2: Syntactic co-occurrences for the word *gracht* 'canal'

To retrieve nearest neighbours, needed for the third-order technique, we computed for each noun a ranked list of most similar words using the methodology described in the two previous sections, i.e. by comparing the weighted feature vector of the headword with all other words in the corpus. We collected the 3 most similar nouns to all nouns. These are the nearest neighbours that will be input to our third-order system.

Now, how do we construct a second-order vector from these nearest neighbours? The cells of the second-order vectors that we want to construct should reflect the similarity between pairs of words. The scores given to the pairs of words by the system do not usually reflect the similarity very well across different headwords and discriminates too little between different nearest neighbours for a given headword.

Instead we used the ranks or rather reversed ranks for a given candidate word. However, the decrease in similarity between the first candidate and the second is not linear. It decreases more rapidly. After inspecting the average decrease in similarity for nearest neighbours, when going down the ranked list, we decided to use a scoring method that is in line with Zipf's law (Zipf, 1949). We decided to attribute similarity scores that are decreasing very rapidly for the first ranks and less as we go down the ranked list of nearest neighbours.

Apart from deciding on the slope of the similarity score we needed to set a start value. We decided to choose a start value according to the highest co-occurrence frequency (in the syntactic co-occurrences) for that headword. So if a headword's

GRACHT 'canal'		
97	gracht	'canal'
48	laan	'avenue'
32	sloot	'ditch'

Figure 3: Nearest neighbours for the word *gracht* 'canal'

highest co-occurrence frequency was 100, a similarity score of 100 is given to the word at the first rank (that is itself) and a score of 50 to the candidate word at the second rank and so on. The intuition between this is that we want to balance the importance given to nearest neighbours and syntactic co-occurrences. The importance of the nearest neighbours will not tresspass the importance of the syntactic co-occurrences.

The highest score will be given to the second-order affinity between a headword and itself. This seems an unnecessary addition, but it is not, because we want *canal* to be similar to words that have *canal* as a second-order affinity as well.

The second-order similarity score (SOSS) for a given headword (h) and a given nearest neighbour (nn) is defined as follows:

$$\textit{SOSS(h,nn)} = \frac{max.freq.of.coocc(h)}{rank(nn)}$$

We have given an example of the second-order feature vector of the word *gracht* 'canal' in Figure 3. As we see the highest score is given to second-order affinity between the headword and the headword itself : *gracht-gracht*. This score is taken from the highest co-occurrence frequency found for the word *gracht* as can be seen in Figure 2. Second-order feature vectors such as given in Figure 3 are constructed for all headwords to be used as input to the third-order technique. For the combined technique we concatenated both types of data. So the input to the combined technique for the word *canal* would be all its syntactic co-occurrences of which a subset is given in Figure 2 plus the three nearest neighbours given in Figure 3.

5 Evaluation

In the following subsections we will first explain how we determined the semantic similarity of the retrieved nearest neighbours (subsection 5.1) and then we will describe the test sets used (subsection 5.2).

5.1 EWN similarity measure and synonyms

Like most researchers in the field of distributional methods we have little choice but to evaluate our work on the resource that we want to enrich. We want to be able to enrich Dutch EuroWordNet (EWN, Vossen (1998)), but at the same time we use it to evaluate on. Especially for Dutch there are not many resources to evaluate semantically related words available.

For each word we collected its k nearest neighbours according to the system. For each pair of words[4] (target word plus one of the nearest neighbours) we calculated the semantic similarity according to EWN. We used the Wu and Palmer measure (Wu and Palmer, 1994) applied to Dutch EWN for computing the semantic similarity between two words.[5] The EWN similarity of a set of word pairs is defined as the average of the similarity between the pairs.

The Wu and Palmer measure for computing the semantic similarity between two words (W1 and W2) in a word net, whose most specific common subsumer (lowest super-ordinate) is W3, is defined as follows:

$$\mathit{Sim(W1,W2)} = \frac{2(D3)}{D1 + D2 + 2(D3)}$$

We computed, D1 (D2) as the distance from W1 (W2) to the lowest common ancestor of W1 and W2, W3. D3 is the distance of that ancestor to the root node.

Some words returned by the system as nearest neighbours cannot be found in EWN. Because counting the words not found in EWN as errors would be too harsh[6] we select the next nearest neighbour that is found in EWN, when encountering a not-found word.

The Wu and Palmer measure gives an indication of the degree of semantic similarity among the retrieved neighbours. The fact that it combines several lexical relations, such as synonymy, hyponymy, an co-hyponymy is an advantage on the one hand, but it is coupled with the disadvantage that it is a rather opaque measure. We have therefore decided to look at one lexical relation in particular: We calculated the percentage of synonyms according to EWN. Note that it is a very strict evaluation and the numbers will therefore be relatively low. Because Dutch EWN is much smaller than Princeton WordNet many synonyms are missing.

		EWN similarity			
		k=1	k=3	k=5	k=10
VLF	2	0.391	0.378	0.364	0.350
	2-3	0.395	0.392	0.376	0.359
	3	0.413	0.412	0.411	0.410
LF	2	0.433	0.408	0.392	0.371
	2-3	0.434	0.417	0.401	0.381
	3	0.437	0.426	0.426	0.428
MF	2	0.644	0.605	0.586	0.555
	2-3	0.646	0.608	0.589	0.561
	3	0.643	0.608	0.589	0.575
HF	2	0.719	0.672	0.645	0.610
	2-3	0.718	0.674	0.645	0.612
	3	0.720	0.670	0.639	0.615

Table 2: EWN similarity several values of k for the four test sets

5.2 Test sets

To evaluate on EWN, we have used four test sets of each 1000 words ranging over four frequency bands: high-frequency, middle frequency, low-frequency, and very-low frequency. For every noun appearing in EWN we have determined its frequency in the 80 million-word corpus of newspaper text. For the high-frequency test set the frequency ranges from 258,253 (*jaar*, 'year') to 2,278 (*scène*, 'scene'). The middle frequency test set has frequencies ranging between 541 (*celstraf*, 'jail sentence') and 364 (*vredesverdrag*, 'peace treaty'). The low-frequency test set has frequencies ranging between 28 (*röntgenonderzoek*, 'x-ray research') and 23 (*vriendenprijs*, 'paltry amount'). For the very low frequency test set the frequency goes from 9 (*slaginstrument* 'percussion instrument') to 8 (*cederhout* 'cedar wood').

[4] If a word is ambiguous according to EWN, i.e. is a member of several synsets, the highest similarity score is used.

[5] This measure correlates well with human judgements (Lin, 1998b) without the need for sense-tagged frequency information, which we believe is not available for Dutch.

[6] Dutch EWN is incomplete. It is about half the size of Princeton WordNet (Fellbaum, 1998). Nearest neighbours that are not found in EWN might be valuable additions that we do not want to penalise the system too much for.

6 Results and discussion

In Table 2 the results of using second-order (2), combined (2+3), and third-order (3) techniques is presented. The average EWN similarity is shown at several values of k. At k=1 the average EWN similarity between the test word and the nearest neighbour at the first rank is calculated. For k=3 we average over the top-three nearest neighbours returned by the system and so on. Results are given for each of the four test sets, the very-low-frequency set (VLF), the low-frequency test set (LF), the middle-frequency test set (MF), and high-frequency test set (HF).

We can easily compare the scores from the second-order technique and the combined technique. The scores for the third-order technique is a little more difficult to compare because, since there is very little data, it is often not possible for all test words to find the number of nearest neighbours given under k. The coverage of the third-order technique is low, especially for the very-low to low-frequency test set. Already at k=1 the number of test word is about 60% and 70% (resp.) of the number of nearest neighbours found when using the second-order technique. For the middle and high-frequency test set the number of nearest neighbours found is comparable, but less for high values of k.

Let us compare the second-order and combined techniques since coverage of these techniques is more comparable.[7] We see that the combined method outperforms the second-order method for almost all test sets. For the high frequency test set there is no difference in performance and for the middle-frequency testset the differences are very small too. The largest improvements are for the very-low-frequency and low-frequency test set. This is expected, since the method was introduced to remedy data sparseness and for these words data sparseness is most severe. We can conclude that exploiting the transitivity of meaning by augmenting the input to the system with nearest neighbours from a previous round results in a higher degree of semantic similarity among very-low and low-frequency words. The differences in performance are small, but we should keep in mind that that EWN similarity does not go from 0 to 1. The random baseline reported in van der Plas (2008), i.e. the score obtained by picking random words from EWN as nearest neighbours of a given target word, is 0.26 at k=5 and a score of 1 is impossible unless all words in the testset have k synonyms.

	Synonyms			
	k=1	k=3	k=5	k=10
HF				
2	143(14.39)	276(9.26)	357(7.18)	461(4.64)
2+3	148(14.89)	275(9.22)	356(7.16)	465(4.68)
3	154(15.54)	259(8.84)	315(6.73)	382(5.26)
MF				
2	105(10.56)	194(6.51)	245(4.93)	312(3.14)
2+3	109(10.97)	200(6.71)	250(5.03)	318(3.20)
3	107(11.38)	173(6.60)	198(5.07)	214(3.95)
LF				
2	33(3.75)	65(2.47)	87(2.00)	108(1.28)
2+3	34(3.86)	73(2.77)	88(2.01)	113(1.32)
3	25(4.01)	41(3.18)	48(3.10)	54(3.20)
VLF				
2	2(0.54)	4(0.36)	8(0.44)	10(0.30)
2+3	2(0.54)	4(0.36)	9(0.49)	10(0.29)
3	2(0.91)	2(0.50)	2(0.44)	2(0.42)

Table 3: Number of synonyms at several values of k for the four test sets

To get a better idea of what is going on we inspected the nearest neighbours that are the output of the system. There seemed to be many more synonyms in the output of the combined method than in the output of the second-order method. Because synonymy is the lexical relation that is at the far end of semantic similarity, it is important to find many synonyms. To quantify our findings we determined the number of synonyms among the nearest neighbours according to EWN.

In Table 3 the number of synonyms as well as the percentage of synonyms found at several values of k is shown.[8]

Our initial findings proved quantifiable. The combined technique (2+3) results in more synonyms. Most surprising are the results for the high-frequency testset. Whereas, based on evaluations with the EWN similarity scores, we believed the method did not do much good for the high-frequency

[7] In fact, the coverage of the combined method is a bit higher, because it combines two types of data, but the differences are not as big as between the third-order and the second-order technique.

[8] At k=n we do not always find n nearest neighbour for all words in the test set. That is the reason for showing both counts and percentages in the table.

Second-order				Combined
cassette	**videoband**	**bandje**	**CDi**	**cassette**
cassette	videoband	bandje	CDi	cassette
videoband	cassette	cassette	DCC	videoband
CDi	videofilm	videoband	CD	bandje

Figure 4: Nearest neighbours for *videoband* 'video tape', *cassette* 'cassette' *bandje* 'tape' and *CDi* 'CDi'

method, we now see that the number of synonyms found is higher when using the combined technique, especially at k=1. This holds for all but one test set. Only for the very low frequency test set there is hardly any difference.

We explained before that coverage of the third-order technique is low. However, we see that the technique results in higher numbers of synonyms found at k=1 for the high-frequency (+11) and the middle-frequency test set (+2). At higher values of k the absolute numbers are smaller for the third-order technique and also for the low and very-low-frequency test set. This is to be expected because the number of nearest neighbours found dramatically decreases, when using a third-order technique on its own. But it is surprising that we are able to extract more synonyms, when using only the two nearest neighbours (plus the headword itself) computed by the system before as input.

Manual inspection showed that what happens is that nearest neighbours that have each other as nearest neighbour are promoted. As can be seen in Figure 4, *cassette* 'cassette' has *videoband* 'video tape', and *CDi* as nearest neighbour. Because CDi has no nearest neighbours in common with *cassette*, except itself, it is demoted in the output of the combined method. The word *bandje* 'tape' has two neighbours in common with *cassette*. *Bandje* is promoted in the output of the combined method.

This finding bring us to work by Lin (1998a), where the author shows that, when selecting only respective nearest neighbours (words that have each other as the one most nearest neighbour), the results are rather good. Our technique incorporates that notion, but is less restricted, especially in the combined technique.

7 Conclusion and future work

Guided by the idea of the transitivity of meaning we have shown that by augmenting syntactic co-occurrences (that are usually input to distributional methods) with nearest neighbours (the output of the system from a previous round) we are able to improve the performance on low- and middle-frequency words with respect to semantic relatedness in general. This result is encouraging, because distributional methods usually perform rather poorly on low- and middle-frequency words. In addition, these are the words that are most sought after, because they are the ones that are missing in existing resources. There is something to be gained for the high-frequency to low-frequency words in addition. The percentage of synonyms found is larger when using combined techniques.

In future work we are planning to implement a more principled way of combining syntactic-co-occurrences and nearest neighbours. The method and results presented here sufficed to support our intuitions, but we believe that more convincing numbers could be attained when fully exploiting the principle. Since the method uses a combination of labelled and unlabelled data (although in our case the labelling is the result of the same unsupervised method and not of manual annotation), we plan to consult the literature on co-training (Blum and Mitchell, 1998). Also, instead of expanding the syntactic co-occurrences of words with their nearest neighbours we could expand them with the syntactic co-occurrences of their nearest neighbours to arrive at more uniform data. Lastly, the technique allows for iteration. We could measure the performance at several iterations.

Acknowledgements

The research leading to these results has received funding from the EU FP7 programme (FP7/2007-2013) under grant agreement nr 216594 (CLASSIC project: www.classic-project.org) and from NWO, the Dutch Organisation for Scientific Research in the framework of the research program for *Interactive Multimedia Information eXtraction*, IMIX.

References

E. Alfonseca and S. Manandhar. 2002. Extending a lexical ontology by a combination of distributional semantics signatures. In *Proceedings of EKAW*.

C. Biemann, S. Bordag, and U. Quasthoff. 2004. Automatic acquisition of paradigmatic relations using iterated co-occurrences. In *Proceedings of LREC*.

A. Blum and T. Mitchell. 1998. Combining labeled and unlabeled data with co-training. In *Proceedings of the 1998 conference on computational learning theory*.

K.W. Church and P. Hanks. 1989. Word association norms, mutual information and lexicography. *Proceedings of the Annual Conference of the Association of Computational Linguistics (ACL)*.

J.R. Curran and M. Moens. 2002. Improvements in automatic thesaurus extraction. In *Proceedings of the Conference on Empirical Methods in Natural Language Processing, EMNLP*, pages 222–229.

J.R. Curran. 2003. *From Distributional to Semantic Similarity*. Ph.D. thesis, University of Edinburgh.

I. Dagan, L. Lee, and F. Pereira. 1999. Similarity-based models of word cooccurrence probabilities. *Machine Learning*, 34(1-3):43–69.

P. Edmonds. 1997. Choosing the word most typical in context using a lexical co-occurrence network. In *Proceedings of the European chapter of the Association for Computational Linguistics*, pages 507–509.

C. Fellbaum. 1998. WordNet, an electronic lexical database. MIT Press.

G. Grefenstette. 1994. Corpus-derived first-, second-, and third-order word affinities. In *Proceedings of Euralex*.

Z.S. Harris. 1968. *Mathematical structures of language*. Wiley.

L. Lee. 1999. Measures of distributional similarity. In *37th Annual Meeting of the Association for Computational Linguistics (ACL)*.

B. Lemaire and G. Denhire. 2006. Effects of high-order co-occurrences on word semantic similarities. *Current Psychology Letters - Behaviour, Brain and Cognition*, 18(1).

D. Lin. 1998a. Automatic retrieval and clustering of similar words. In *Proceedings of COLING/ACL*.

D. Lin. 1998b. An information-theoretic definition of similarity. In *Proceedings of the 15th International Conference on Machine Learning*.

M. Moortgat, I. Schuurman, and T. van der Wouden. 2000. CGN syntactische annotatie. Internal Project Report Corpus Gesproken Nederlands, available from `http://lands.let.kun.nl/cgn`.

R.J.F. Ordelman. 2002. Twente nieuws corpus (TwNC). Parlevink Language Techonology Group. University of Twente.

P. Resnik. 1993. Selection and information. Unpublished doctoral thesis, University of Pennsylvania.

H. Schütze and M. Walsh. 2008. A graph-theoretic model of lexical syntactic acquisition. In *Proceedings of EMNLP*.

A. Tversky and I. Gati, 1978. *Cognition and Categorisation*, chapter Studies of similarity, pages 81–98. Erlbaum.

L. van der Plas and G. Bouma. 2005. Syntactic contexts for finding semantically similar words. In *Proceedings of Computational Linguistics in the Netherlands (CLIN)*.

L. van der Plas. 2008. *Automatic lexico-semantic acquisition for question answering*. Ph.D. thesis, University of Groningen.

G. van Noord. 2006. At last parsing is now operational. In *Actes de la 13eme Conference sur le Traitement Automatique des Langues Naturelles*.

P. Vossen. 1998. EuroWordNet a multilingual database with lexical semantic networks.

J. Weeds and W. Weir. 2005. Co-occurrence retrieval: A flexible framework for lexical distributional similarity. *Computational Linguistics*, 31(4):439–475.

J. Weeds. 2003. *Measures and Applications of Lexical Distributional Similarity*. Ph.D. thesis, University of Sussex.

D. Widdows. 2004. *Geometry and Meaning*. Center for the Study of Language and Information/SRI.

Z. Wu and M. Palmer. 1994. Verb semantics and lexical selection. In *Proceedings of the Annual Meeting of the Association for Computational Linguistics (ACL)*.

G.K. Zipf. 1949. *Human behavior and the principle of the least effort*. Addison-Wesley.

Using DEDICOM for Completely Unsupervised Part-of-Speech Tagging

Peter A. Chew, Brett W. Bader
Sandia National Laboratories
P. O. Box 5800, MS 1012
Albuquerque, NM 87185-1012, USA
{pchew,bwbader}@sandia.gov

Alla Rozovskaya
Department of Computer Science
University of Illinois
Urbana, IL 61801, USA
rozovska@illinois.edu

Abstract

A standard and widespread approach to part-of-speech tagging is based on Hidden Markov Models (HMMs). An alternative approach, pioneered by Schütze (1993), induces parts of speech from scratch using singular value decomposition (SVD). We introduce DEDICOM as an alternative to SVD for part-of-speech induction. DEDICOM retains the advantages of SVD in that it is completely unsupervised: no prior knowledge is required to induce either the tagset or the associations of types with tags. However, unlike SVD, it is also fully compatible with the HMM framework, in that it can be used to estimate emission- and transition-probability matrices which can then be used as the input for an HMM. We apply the DEDICOM method to the CONLL corpus (CONLL 2000) and compare the output of DEDICOM to the part-of-speech tags given in the corpus, and find that the correlation (almost 0.5) is quite high. Using DEDICOM, we also estimate part-of-speech ambiguity for each type, and find that these estimates correlate highly with part-of-speech ambiguity as measured in the original corpus (around 0.88). Finally, we show how the output of DEDICOM can be evaluated and compared against the more familiar output of supervised HMM-based tagging.

1 Introduction

Traditionally, part-of-speech tagging has been approached either in a rule-based fashion, or stochastically. Harris (1962) was among the first to develop algorithms of the former type. The rule-based approach relies on two elements: a dictionary to assign possible parts of speech to each word, and a list of hand-written rules – which must be painstakingly developed for each new language or domain – to disambiguate tokens in context. Stochastic taggers, on the other hand, avoid the need for hand-written rules by tabulating probabilities of types and part-of-speech tags (which must be gathered from a tagged training corpus), and applying a special case of Bayesian inference (usually, Hidden Markov Models [HMMs]) to disambiguate tokens in context. The latter approach was pioneered by Stolz et al. (1965) and Bahl and Mercer (1976), and became widely known through the work of e.g. Church (1988) and DeRose (1988).

A third and more recent approach, known as 'distributional tagging' and exemplified by Schütze (1993, 1995) and Biemann (2006), aims to eliminate the need for both hand-written rules *and* a tagged training corpus, since the latter may not be available for every language or domain. Distributional tagging is fully-unsupervised, unlike the two traditional approaches described above. Schütze suggests analyzing the distributional patterns of words by forming a term adjacency matrix, then subjecting that matrix to Singular Value Decomposition (SVD) to reveal latent dimensions. He shows that in the reduced-dimensional space implied by SVD, tokens do indeed cluster intuitively by part-of-speech; and that if context is taken into account, something akin to part-of-speech tagging

Proceedings of the NAACL HLT Workshop on Unsupervised and Minimally Supervised Learning of Lexical Semantics, pages 54–62,
Boulder, Colorado, June 2009.

can be achieved. Whereas the performance of stochastic taggers is generally sub-optimal when the domain of the training data differs from that of the test data, distributional tagging sidesteps this problem, since each corpus can be considered in its own right. Schütze (1995) notes two general drawbacks of distributional tagging methods: the performance is relatively modest compared to that of supervised methods; and languages with rich morphology may pose a challenge.[1]

In this paper, we present an alternative unsupervised approach to distributional tagging. Instead of SVD, we use a dimensionality reduction technique known as DEDICOM, which has various advantages over the SVD-based approach. Principal among these is that, even though no pre-tagged corpus is required, DEDICOM can easily be used as input to a HMM-based approach (and the two share linear-algebraic similarities, as we will make clear in section 4). Although our empirical results, like those of Schütze (1995), are perhaps still relatively modest, the fact that a clearer connection exists between DEDICOM and HMMs than between SVD and HMMs gives us good reason to believe that with further refinements, DEDICOM may be able to give us 'the best of both worlds' in many respects: the benefits of avoiding the need for a pre-tagged corpus, with empirical results approaching those of HMM-based tagging.

In the following sections, we introduce DEDICOM, describe its applicability to the part-of-speech tagging problem, and outline its connections to the standard HMM-based approach to tagging. We evaluate the use of DEDICOM on the CONLL 2000 shared task data, discuss the results and suggest avenues for improvement.

2 DEDICOM

DEDICOM, which stands for 'DEcomposition into DIrectional COMponents', is a linear-algebraic decomposition method attributable to Harshman (1978) which has been used to analyze matrices of asymmetrical directional relationships between objects or persons. Early on, the technique was applied by Harshman et al. (1982) to the analysis of two types of marketing data: 'free associations' – how often one phrase (describing hair shampoo) evokes another in the minds of survey respondents, and 'car switching data' – how often people switch from one to another of 16 car types. Both datasets are asymmetric and directional: in the first dataset, for example, the phrase 'body' (referring to shampoo) evoked the phrase 'fullness' twice as often in the minds of respondents as 'fullness' evoked 'body'. Likewise, the data from Harshman et al. (1982) show that in the given period, 3,820 people switched from 'midsize import' cars to 'midsize domestic' cars, but only 2,140 switches were made in the reverse direction. Another characteristic of these 'asymmetric directional' datasets is that they can be represented in square matrices. For example, the raw car switching data can be represented in a 16 × 16 matrix, since there are 16 car types.

The objective of DEDICOM, which can be compared to that of SVD, is to factorize the raw data matrices into a lower-dimensional space identifying underlying, idealized directional patterns in the data. For example, while there are 16 car types in the raw car switching data, Harshman shows that under a 4-dimensional DEDICOM analysis, these can be 'boiled down' to the basic types 'plain large-midsize', 'specialty', 'fancy large', and 'small' – and that patterns of switching among these more basic types can then be identified.

If X represents the original $n \times n$ matrix of asymmetric relationships, and a general entry x_{ij} in X represents the strength of the directed relationship of object i to object j, then the single-domain DEDICOM model[2] can be written as follows:

$$X = ARA^T + E \qquad (1)$$

where A denotes an $n \times q$ matrix of weights of the n observed objects in q dimensions (where $q < n$), and R is a dense $q \times q$ asymmetric matrix expressing the directional relationships between the q dimensions or basic types. A^T is simply the transpose

[1] We note the latter is also true for languages in which word order is relatively free – usually the same languages as those with rich morphology. While English word order is significantly constrained by part-of-speech categorizations, this is not as true of, say, Russian. Thus, an adjacency matrix formed from a Russian corpus is likely to be less informative about part-of-speech classifications as one formed from an English corpus. Quite possibly, this is as much of a limitation for DEDICOM as it is for SVD.

[2] There is a dual-domain DEDICOM model, which is also described in Harshman (1978). The dual-domain DEDICOM model is not relevant to our discussion, and thus it will not be mentioned further. References in this paper to 'DEDICOM' are to be understood as references in shorthand to 'single-domain DEDICOM'.

of A, and E is a matrix of error terms. Our objective is to minimize E, so we can also write:

$$X \approx ARA^T \qquad (2)$$

As noted by Harshman (1978: 209), the fact that A appears on both the left and right of R means that the data is described 'in terms of asymmetric relations among a *single* set of things' – in other words, when objects are on the receiving end of the directional relationships, they are still of the same type as those on the initiating end.

One difference between DEDICOM and SVD is that there is no unique solution: either A or R can be scaled or rotated without changing the goodness of fit, so long as the inverse operation is applied to the other. For example, if we let $\hat{A} = AD$, where D is any diagonal scaling matrix (or, more generally, any nonsingular matrix), then we can write

$$X \approx ARA^T = \hat{A}D^{-1}RD^{-1}\hat{A}^T \qquad (3)$$

since $\hat{A}^T = (AD)^T = DA^T$

(In our application, we constrain A and R to be nonnegative as noted below.)

To our knowledge, there have been no applications of DEDICOM to date in computational linguistics. This is in contrast to SVD, which has been extensively used for text analysis (for applications other than unsupervised part-of-speech tagging, see Baeza-Yates and Ribeiro-Neto 1999).

3 Applicability of DEDICOM to part-of-speech tagging

Schütze's (1993) key insight is that – at least in English – adjacencies between types are a good guide to their grammatical functions. That insight can be leveraged by applying either SVD or DEDICOM to a type-by-type adjacency matrix. With DEDICOM, however, we add the constraint (already stated) that the types are a 'single set of things': whether a type 'precedes' or 'follows' – i.e., whether it is in a row or a column of the matrix – does not affect its grammatical function. This constraint is as it should be, and, to our knowledge, sets DEDICOM apart from all previous unsupervised approaches including those of Schütze (1993, 1995) and Biemann (2006).

Given any corpus containing *n* types and *k* tokens, we can let X be an $n \times n$ token-adjacency matrix. Let each entry x_{ij} in X denote the number of times in the corpus that type *i* immediately precedes type *j*. X is thus a matrix of bigram frequencies. It follows that the sum of the elements of X equals $k - 1$ (because the first token in the corpus is preceded by nothing, and the last token is followed by nothing). Any given row sum of X (the type frequency corresponding to the particular row) will equal the corresponding column sum, except if the type happens to occur in the first or last position in the corpus. X will be asymmetric, since the frequency of bigram *ij* is clearly not the same as that of bigram *ji* for all *i* and *j*.

It can be seen, therefore, that our X represents asymmetric directional data, very similar to the data analyzed in Harshman (1978) and Harshman et al. (1982). If we fit the DEDICOM model to our X matrix, then we obtain an A matrix which represents types by latent classes, and an R matrix which represents directional relationships between latent classes. We can think of the latent classes as induced parts of speech.

With SVD, we believe that the orthogonality of the reduced-dimensional features militates against any attempt to correlate these features with parts of speech. From a linguistic point of view, there is no reason to believe that parts of speech are orthogonal to one another in any sense. For example, nouns and adjectives (traditionally classified together as 'nominals') seem to share more in common with one another than nouns and verbs. With DEDICOM, this is not an issue, because the columns of A are not required to be mutually orthogonal to one another, unlike the left and right singular vectors from SVD.

Thus, the A matrix from DEDICOM shows how strongly associated each type is with the different induced parts of speech; we would expect types which are ambiguous (such as 'claims', which can be either a noun or a verb) to have high loadings on more than one column in A. Again, if the classes correlate with parts of speech, the R matrix will show the latent patterns of adjacency between different parts of speech.

4 Connections between DEDICOM and HMM-based tagging

For any HMM, two components are necessary: a set of emission probabilities and a set of transition probabilities. Applying this framework to part-of-speech tagging, the tags are conceived of as the hidden layer of the HMM and the tokens (each of which is associated with a type) as the visible layer. The emission probabilities are then the probabilities of types given the tags, and the transition probabilities are the probabilities of the tags given the preceding tags. If these probabilities are known, then there are algorithms (such as the Viterbi algorithm) to determine the most likely sequence of tags given the visible sequence of types.

In the case of supervised learning, we obtain the emission and transition probabilities by observing actual frequencies in a tagged corpus. Suppose our corpus, as previously discussed, consists of *n* types and *k* tokens. Since we are dealing with supervised learning, the number of the tags in the tagset is also known: we denote this number *q*. Now, the observed frequencies can be represented, respectively, as $n \times q$ and $q \times q$ matrices: we denote these A* and R*. Each entry a_{ij} in A* denotes the number of times type *i* is associated with tag *j*, and each entry r_{ij} in R* denotes the number of times tag *j* immediately follows tag *i*. Moreover, we know some other properties of A* and R*:

- the respective sums of the elements of A* and R* are equal to $k - 1$;
- each row sum of A* ($\sum_{x=1}^{q} a_{ix}$) corresponds to the frequency in the corpus of type *i*;
- each column sum of A*, as well as the corresponding row and column sums of R*, are the frequencies of the given tags in the corpus (for all *j*, $\sum_{x=1}^{q} a_{xj} = \sum_{x=1}^{q} r_{xj} = \sum_{x=1}^{q} r_{jx}$).

If A* and R* contain frequencies, however, we must perform a matrix operation to obtain transition and emission *probabilities* for use in an HMM-based tagger. In effect, A* must be made column-stochastic, and R* must be made row-stochastic. Since the column sums of A* equal the respective row sums of R*, this can be achieved by post-multiplying both A* and R* by D_A, where D_A is a diagonal scaling matrix containing the inverses of the column sums of A (or equivalently, the row sums of R). Then the matrix of emission probabilities is given by A^*D_A, and the matrix of transition probabilities by R^*D_A.

We can now make the connection to DEDICOM explicit. Let $A = A^*D_A$ and $R = R^*$, then we can rewrite (2) as follows:

$$X \approx ARA^T = (A^*D_A)\, R^*\, (A^*D_A)^T \quad (4)$$

$$X \approx A^*D_A\, R^*D_A\, A^{*T} \quad (5)$$

In other words, for any corpus we may compute a probabilistic representation of the type adjacency matrix X (which will contain *expected* frequencies comparable to the *actual* frequencies) by multiplying the emission probability matrix A^*D_A, the transition probability matrix R^*D_A, and the type-by-tag frequency matrix A*. (Presumably, the closer the approximation, the better the tagging in the training set actually factorizes the true directional relationships.)

Conversely, for fully unsupervised tagging, we can fit the DEDICOM model to the type adjacency matrix X. The resulting A matrix contains estimates of what the tags *should* be (if a tagged training corpus is unavailable), as well as the emission probability of each type given each tag, and the resulting R matrix is the corresponding transition probability matrix given those tags. In this case, a column-stochastic A can be used directly as the emission probability matrix, and we simply make R* row-stochastic to obtain the matrix of transition probabilities. The only difference then between the output of the fully-unsupervised DEDICOM/HMM tagger and that of a supervised HMM tagger is that in the first case, the 'tags' are numeric indices representing the corresponding column of A, and in the second case, they are the members of the tagset used in the training data.

The fact that emission and transition probabilities (or at least something very like them) are a natural by-product of DEDICOM sets DEDICOM apart from Schütze's SVD-based approach, and is for us a significant reason which recommends the use of DEDICOM.

5 Evaluation

For all evaluation described here, we used the CONLL 2000 shared task data (CONLL 2000). This English-language newswire corpus consists of 19,440 types and 259,104 tokens (including punctuation marks as separate types/tokens). Each token is associated with a part-of-speech tag and a chunk tag, although we did not use the chunk tags in the work described here. The tags are from a 44-item tagset. The CONLL 2000 tags against which we measure our own results are in fact assigned by the Brill tagger (Brill 1992), and while these may not correlate perfectly with those that would have been assigned by a human linguist, we believe that the correlation is likely to be good enough to allow for an informative evaluation of our method.

Before discussing the evaluation of unsupervised DEDICOM, let us briefly reconsider the similarities of DEDICOM to the supervised HMM model in the light of actual data in the CONLL corpus. We stated in (5) that $X \approx A^*D_AR^*D_AA^{*T}$. For the CONLL 2000 tagged data, A* is a 19,440 × 44 matrix and R* is a 44 × 44 matrix. Using A^*D_A and R^*D_A as emission- and transition-probability matrices within a standard HMM (where the entire CONLL 2000 corpus is treated as both training and test data), we obtained a tagging accuracy of 95.6%. By multiplying $A^*D_AR^*D_AA^{*T}$, we expect to obtain a matrix approximating X, the table of bigram frequencies. This is indeed what we found: it will be apparent from Table 1 that the top 10 expected bigram frequencies based on this matrix multiplication are generally quite close to actual frequencies. Moreover, the sum of the elements in $A^*D_AR^*D_AA^{*T}$ is equal to the sum of the elements in X, and if we let E be the matrix of error terms ($X - A^*D_AR^*D_AA^{*T}$), then we find that $||E||$ (the Frobenius norm of E) is 38.764% of $||X||$ - in other words, $A^*D_AR^*D_AA^{*T}$ accounts for just over 60% of the data in X.

Type 1	**Type 2**	**Actual frequency**	**Expected frequency**
of	the	1,421.000	1,202.606
in	the	1,213.000	875.822
for	the	553.000	457.067
to	the	445.000	415.524
on	the	439.000	271.528
the	company	383.000	105.794
a	share	371.000	32.447
that	the	315.000	258.679
and	the	302.000	296.737
to	be	285.000	499.315

Table 1. Actual versus expected frequencies for 10 most common bigrams in CONLL 2000 corpus

Having confirmed that there exists an A ($=A^*D_A$) and R (=R*) which both satisfies the DEDICOM model and can be used directly within a HMM-based tagger to achieve satisfactory results, we now consider whether A and R can be estimated if no tagged training set is available.

We start, therefore, from X, the square 19,440 × 19,440 (sparse) matrix of raw bigram frequencies from the CONLL 2000 data. Using Matlab and the Tensor Toolbox (Bader and Kolda 2006, 2007), we computed the best rank-44 non-negative DEDICOM[3] decomposition of this matrix using the 2-way version of the ASALSAN algorithm presented in Bader et al. (2007), which is based on iteratively improving random initial guesses for A and R. As with SVD, the rank of the decomposition can be selected by the user; we chose 44 since that was known to be the number of items in the CONLL 2000 tagset, but a lower number could be selected for a coarser-grained part-of-speech analysis. Ultimately, perhaps the best way to determine the optimal rank would be to evaluate different options within a larger end-to-end system, for example an information retrieval system; this, however, was beyond our scope in this study.

As already mentioned, there are indeterminacies of rotation and scale in DEDICOM. As Harshman et al. (1982: 211) point out, 'when the columns of A are standardized... the R matrix can then be interpreted as expressing relationships among the dimensions in the same units as the original data.

That is, the R matrix can be interpreted as a matrix of the same kind as the original data matrix X, but describing the relations among the latent aspects of the phrases, rather than the phrases themselves'. Thus, if DEDICOM is constrained so that A is column-stochastic (which is required in any case of the matrix of emission probabilities), then the sum of the elements in R should approximate the sum of the elements in X. R is therefore comparable to R* (with some provisos which shall be enumerated below), and to obtain the row-stochastic transition-probability matrix, we simply multiply R by a diagonal matrix D_R whose elements are the inverses of R's row sums.

[3] Non-negative DEDICOM imposes the constraint not present in Harshman (1978, 1982) that all entries in A and R must be non-negative. This constraint is appropriate in the present case, since the entries in A* and R* (and of course the probabilities in A*D and R*D) are by definition non-negative.

	1	2	3	4	5	6	7	8	9	10	11	12	13	14	15	16	17	18	19	20
#	0	0	0	6	0	0	0	0	0	4	0	0	0	0	0	0	0	0	0	0
$	0	29	0	211	0	2	0	1	1	80	0	0	0	0	0	1	0	3	0	27
"	0	11	0	81	0	8	7	0	2	106	0	2	0	0	0	6	0	1	0	45
(	6	9	0	2	9	3	0	4	10	0	14	0	0	1	0	0	0	0	3	0
)	4	3	0	4	37	0	9	0	8	0	2	0	0	0	0	0	0	0	0	0
,	1	216	0	951	14	117	35	2	6	461	0	7	0	0	0	38	0	12	0	376
!	0	0	0	0	0	0	0	0	0	0	0	0	0	0	0	0	0	0	0	0
-	0	12	0	75	2	9	4	0	0	62	0	0	0	0	0	1	0	3	0	36
`	0	16	0	101	3	5	3	3	0	124	0	2	0	0	0	6	0	2	0	28
coordinating conjunction	2	6	1	40	45	3	0	0	397	14	120	7	283	161	0	0	1	0	34	8
cardinal number	606	301	102	81	302	1	7	85	67	1	277	0	29	27	16	15	20	0	0	4
determiner	21	15	3,048	6	85	12	0	70	75	6	79	2	0	81	88	0	685	1	3	7
existential there	0	0	0	1	19	0	0	0	11	0	4	0	0	20	0	0	0	0	0	0
foreign word	0	2	0	2	0	0	0	0	0	0	0	0	0	0	0	0	0	0	0	0
preposition/subordinating conjunct	60	60	16	9	198	1,819	2	34	173	42	59	736	776	152	2	0	10	23	519	23
adjective	110	1,509	511	66	69	12	79	231	62	41	96	1	7	59	113	15	27	1	0	15
adjective, comparative	8	87	35	4	8	0	15	8	1	4	5	0	0	1	6	1	8	0	0	0
adjective, superlative	1	64	7	0	0	0	0	3	0	5	3	0	0	4	1	0	0	0	0	1
modal	4	41	8	35	333	0	0	0	41	0	1	0	1	1	0	0	0	0	0	1
noun, singular or mass	1,219	3,706	256	330	155	42	489	357	54	144	162	1	7	43	23	69	11	27	3	43
proper noun, singular	845	1,529	388	95	538	14	39	391	378	46	291	0	1	118	58	59	71	7	0	6
proper noun, plural	33	65	1	6	12	2	0	3	3	5	1	0	0	0	0	0	0	0	0	0
noun, plural	945	1,284	51	101	119	17	281	102	78	75	78	0	19	19	11	52	4	7	1	11
predeterminer	0	2	0	0	0	7	0	0	0	0	0	0	1	0	0	0	0	0	0	0
possessive ending	0	52	0	392	0	15	0	0	0	4	0	0	0	0	0	2	0	0	0	3
personal pronoun	62	11	0	1	98	3	0	22	333	0	201	0	0	67	2	3	8	0	0	6
possessive pronoun	11	5	75	0	0	0	0	330	0	0	0	0	0	0	15	0	4	0	0	0
adverb	155	169	39	94	359	21	81	17	146	13	115	5	40	87	2	8	7	0	1	13
adverb, comparative	10	19	11	13	13	0	0	0	0	0	1	0	0	0	2	2	0	0	0	0
adverb, superlative	0	38	0	0	0	0	0	0	0	0	9	0	0	2	6	0	0	0	0	0
particle	0	1	0	0	0	0	0	0	0	0	0	0	3	0	0	0	0	0	0	9
*	0	0	0	0	0	0	0	0	0	0	0	0	0	0	0	0	0	0	0	0
to	1	30	0	0	810	70	0	0	13	0	3	11	266	0	0	0	0	0	22	0
interjection	1	0	0	0	1	0	0	0	0	0	0	0	0	0	0	0	0	0	0	0
verb, base form	49	50	88	886	6	87	106	7	4	26	4	5	20	2	2	19	1	6	17	5
verb, past tense	148	62	17	127	171	84	182	3	118	52	79	21	101	12	0	15	1	5	59	21
verb, gerund/past participle	37	105	102	22	20	72	45	49	38	29	50	25	54	31	6	6	5	2	18	7
verb, past participle	105	164	58	18	22	68	294	17	21	59	67	5	44	9	2	14	4	8	7	29
verb, sing. present, non-3d	25	44	22	179	87	34	64	2	25	47	3	0	18	0	0	5	0	1	2	5
verb, 3rd person sing. present	40	54	12	145	40	48	74	0	125	27	26	3	81	5	1	5	2	4	4	4
wh-determiner	0	0	1	0	7	6	0	0	15	9	17	0	0	66	0	0	1	0	16	0
wh-pronoun	0	0	0	0	3	1	0	4	77	6	0	0	0	14	5	0	1	0	0	0
possessive wh-pronoun	0	0	0	0	0	0	0	0	0	0	1	0	0	2	0	0	0	0	0	0
wh-adverb	0	0	0	0	0	3	0	2	10	0	22	7	18	11	1	0	0	0	14	0

Table 2. Partial confusion matrix of gold-standard tags against DEDICOM-induced tags for CONLL 2000 dataset

With A as an emission-probability matrix and RD_R as a transition-probability matrix, we now have all that is needed for an HMM-based tagger to estimate the most likely sequence of 'tags' given the corpus. However, since the 'tags' here are numerical indices, as mentioned, to evaluate the output we must look at the correlation between these 'tags' and the gold-standard tags given in the CONLL 2000 data. One way this can be done is by presenting a 44 × 44 confusion matrix (of gold-standard tags against induced tags), and then measuring the correlation coefficient (Pearson's R) between that matrix and the 'idealized' confusion matrix in which each induced tag corresponds to one and only one 'gold standard' tag. Using A and RD_R as the input to a HMM-based tagger, we tagged the CONLL 2000 dataset with induced tags and obtained the confusion matrix shown in Table 2 (owing to space constraints, only the first 20 columns are shown). The correlation between this matrix and the equivalent diagonalized 'ideal' matrix is in fact 0.4942, which is significantly higher than could have occurred by chance.

It should be noted that a lack of correlation between the induced tags and the gold standard tags can be attributed to at least two independent factors. The first, of course, is any inability of the DEDICOM model to fit the particular problem and data. Clearly, this is undesirable. The other factor to be borne in mind, which works to DEDICOM's favor, is that the DEDICOM model could yield an A and R which factorize the data more optimally than the A*D and R* implied by the gold-standard tags. There are three methods we can use to try and tease apart these competing explanations of the results, two quantitative and the other subjective. Quantitatively, we can compare the respective error matrices E. We have already mentioned that

$$\frac{\| X - A^* D_A R^* D_A A^{*T} \|}{\| X \|} \approx 0.38764 \quad (6)$$

Similarly, using the A and R from DEDICOM we can compute

$$\frac{\| X - ARA^T \|}{\| X \|} \approx 0.24078 \quad (7)$$

The fact that the error is lower in the second case implies that DEDICOM allows us to find a part-of-speech 'factorization' of the data which fits better even than the gold standard, although again there are some caveats to this; we will return to these in the discussion.

Another way to evaluate the output of DEDICOM is by comparing the number of part-of-speech tags for a type in the gold standard to the number of classes in the A matrix with which the type is strongly associated. We test this by measuring the Pearson correlation between the two variables. First, we compute the average number of part-of-speech tags per type using the gold standard. We refer to this value as *ambiguity coefficient*; for the CONLL dataset, this is 1.05. Because A is dense, if we count all non-zero columns for a type in the A matrix as possible classes, we obtain a much higher ambiguity coefficient. We therefore set a threshold and consider only those columns whose values exceed a certain threshold. The threshold is selected so that the ambiguity coefficient of the A matrix is the same as that of the gold standard. For a given type, every column with a value exceeding the threshold is counted as a possible class for that type. We then compute the Pearson correlation coefficient between the number of classes for a type in the A matrix and the number of part-of speech tags for that type in the CONLL dataset as provided by the Brill tagger. We obtained a correlation coefficient of 0.88, which shows that there is indeed a high correlation between the induced tags and the gold standard tags obtained with DEDICOM.

Finally, we can evaluate the output subjectively by looking at the content of the A matrix. For each 'tag' (column) in A, the 'types' (rows) can be listed in decreasing order of their weighting in A. This gives us an idea of which types are most characteristic of which tags, and whether the grouping into tags makes any intuitive sense. These results (for selected tags only, owing to limitations of space) are given in Table 3.

Many groupings in Table 3 do make sense: for example, the fourth tag is clearly associated with verbs, while the two types with significant weightings for tag 2 are both determiners. By referring back to Table 2, we can see that many tokens in the CONLL 2000 dataset tagged as verbs are indeed tagged by the DEDICOM tagger as 'tag 4', while many determiners are tagged as 'tag 3'. To understand where a *lack* of correlation may arise, however, it is informative to look at apparent anomalies in the A matrix. For example, it can be seen from Table 3 that 'new', an adjective, is grouped in the third tag with 'a' and 'the' (and ranking above 'an'). Although not in agreement with the CONLL 2000 'gold standard' tagging, the idea that determiners are a type of adjective is in fact in accordance with traditional English grammar. Here, the grouping of 'new', 'a' and 'the' can be explained by the distributional similarities (all precede nouns). It should also be emphasized that the A matrix is essentially a 'soft clustering' of types (meaning that types can belong to more than one cluster). Thus, for example, 'u.s.' (the abbreviation for United States) appears under both tag 2 (which appears to have high loadings for nouns) and tag 8 (with high loadings for adjectives).

We have alluded above in passing to possible methods for improving the results of the DEDICOM analysis. One would be to pre-process the data differently. Here, a variety of options are available which maintain a generally unsupervised approach (one example is to avoid treating punctuation as tokens). However, variations in pre-processing are beyond the scope of this paper.

Tag	Top 10 types (by weight) with weightings								
1	million	share	said	.	year	billion	inc.	corp.	years	quarter
	0.0246	0.0146	0.0129	0.0098	0.0088	0.0069	0.0064	0.0061	0.0058	0.0054
2	company	u.s.	new	first	market	share	year	stock	.	government
	0.0264	0.0136	0.0113	0.0095	0.0086	0.0086	0.0079	0.0077	0.0065	0.006
3	the	a	new	an	other	its	any	addition	their	1988
	0.2889	0.1194	0.0121	0.0094	0.0092	0.0085	0.0067	0.0062	0.0062	0.0057
...										
8	the	its	his	about	those	their	all	u.s.	.	this
	0.0935	0.0462	0.0208	0.0160	0.0096	0.0095	0.0088	0.0077	0.0074	0.0071
...										

Table 3. Type weightings in A matrix, by tag

Another method would be to constrain DEDICOM so that the output more closely models the characteristics of A* and R*, the emission- and transition-probability matrices obtained from a tagged training set. In particular, there is one important constraint on R* which is not replicated in R: the constraint mentioned above that for all *j*, $\sum_{x=1}^{q} r_{xj} = \sum_{x=1}^{q} r_{jx}$. We note that this constraint can be satisfied by Sinkhorn balancing (Sinkhorn 1964)[4], although it remains to be seen how the constraint on R can best be incorporated into the DEDICOM architecture. Assuming that A is column-stochastic, another desirable constraint is that the rows of $A(D_R)^{-1}$ should sum to the same as the rows of X (the respective type frequencies). With the implementation of these (and any other) constraints, one would expect the fit of DEDICOM to the data to worsen (cf. (6) and (7) above), but incurring this cost could be worthwhile if the payoff were somehow linguistically interesting (for example, if it turned out we could achieve a much higher correlation to gold-standard tagging).

6 Conclusion

In this paper, we have introduced DEDICOM, an analytical technique which to our knowledge has not previously been used in computational linguistics, and applied it to the problem of completely unsupervised part-of-speech tagging. Theoretically, the model has features which recommend it over other previous approaches to unsupervised tagging, specifically SVD. Principal among the advantages is the compatibility of DEDICOM with the standard HMM-based approach to part-of-speech tagging, but another significant advantage is the fact that types are treated as 'a single set of objects' regardless of whether they occupy the first or second position in a bigram.

By applying DEDICOM to a tagged dataset, we have shown that there is a significant correlation between the tags induced by unsupervised, DEDICOM-based tagging, and the pre-existing gold-standard tags. This points both to an inherent validity in the gold-standard tags (as a reasonable factorization of the data) and to the fact that DEDICOM appears promising as a method of inducing tags in cases where no gold standard is available.

We have also shown that the factors of DEDICOM are interesting in their own right: our tests show that the A matrix (similar to an emission-probability matrix) models type part-of-speech ambiguity well. Using insights from DEDICOM, we have also shown how linear algebraic techniques may be used to estimate the fit of a given part-of-speech factorization (whether induced or manually created) to a given dataset, by comparing actual versus expected bigram frequencies.

In summary, it appears that DEDICOM is a promising way forward for bridging the gap between unsupervised and supervised approaches to part-of-speech tagging, and we are optimistic that with further refinements to DEDICOM (such as the addition of appropriate constraints), more insight will be gained on how DEDICOM may most profitably be used to improve part-of-speech tagging when few pre-existing resources (such as tagged corpora) are available.

Acknowledgements

We are grateful to Danny Dunlavy for contributing his thoughts to this work.

Sandia is a multiprogram laboratory operated by Sandia Corporation, a Lockheed Martin Company, for the United States Department of Energy's National Nuclear Security Administration under contract DE-AC04-94AL85000.

[4] It is also worth noting that Sinkhorn was motivated by the same problem which concerns us, that of estimating a transition-probability matrix for a Markov model.

References

Brett W. Bader, Richard A. Harshman, and Tamara G. Kolda. 2007. Temporal analysis of semantic graphs using ASALSAN. In *Proceedings of the 7th IEEE International Conference on Data Mining*, 33-42.

Brett W. Bader and Tamara G. Kolda. 2006. Efficient MATLAB Computations with Sparse and Factored Tensors. *Technical Report SAND2006-7592*, Sandia National Laboratories, Albuquerque, NM and Livermore, CA.

Brett W. Bader and Tamara G. Kolda. 2007. The MATLAB Tensor Toolbox, version 2.2. http://csmr.ca.sandia.gov/~tgkolda/TensorToolbox/.

Ricardo Baeza-Yates and Berthier Ribeiro-Neto. 1999. *Modern Information Retrieval*. New York: ACM Press.

L. R. Bahl and R. L. Mercer. 1976. Part of speech assignment by a statistical decision algorithm. In *Proceedings of the IEEE International Symposium on Information Theory*, 88-89.

C. Biemann. 2006. Unsupervised part-of-speech tagging employing efficient graph clustering. In *Proceedings of the COLING/ACL 2006 Student Research Workshop*, 7-12.

E. Brill. 1992. A simple rule-based part of speech tagger. In *Proceedings of the Third Conference on Applied Natural Language Processing*, 152-155.

K. W. Church. 1988. A stochastic parts program and noun phrase parser for unrestricted text. In *ANLP 1988*, 136-143.

CONLL 2000. Shared task data. Retrieved Dec. 1, 2008 from http://www.cnts.ua.ac.be/conll2000/chunking/.

S. J. DeRose. 1988. Grammatical category disambiguation by statistical optimization. *Computational Linguistics* 14, 31-39.

Harris, Z. S. 1962. *String Analysis of Sentence Structure*. Mouton: The Hague.

Richard Harshman. 1978. Models for Analysis of Asymmetrical Relationships Among N Objects or Stimuli. *Paper presented at the First Joint Meeting of the Psychometric Society and The Society for Mathematical Psychology*. Hamilton, Canada.

Richard Harshman, Paul Green, Yoram Wind, and Margaret Lundy. 1982. A Model for the Analysis of Asymmetric Data in Marketing Research. *Marketing Science* 1(2), 205-242.

Hinrich Schütze. 1993. Part-of-Speech Induction from Scratch. In *Proceedings of the 31st Annual Meeting of the Association for Computational Linguistics*, 251-258.

Hinrich Schütze. 1995. Distributional Part-of-Speech Tagging. In *Proceedings of the 7th Conference of the European Chapter of the Association for Computational Linguistics*, 141-148.

Richard Sinkhorn. 1964. A Relationship Between Arbitrary Positive Matrices and Doubly Stochastic Matrices. *The Annals of Mathematical Statistics* 35(2), 876-879.

W. S. Stolz, P. H. Tannenbaum, and F. V. Carstensen. 1965. A stochastic approach to the grammatical coding of English. *Communications of the ACM* 8(6), 399-405.